I Dare To Heal With Spiritual Power

I Dare To Heal With Spiritual Power

Joel Vorensky

To order additional copies of this book, contact:
Xlibris Corporation
1-888-795-4274
www.Xlibris.com
Orders@Xlibris.com
26209

REVIEWS

Joel Vorensky's book, I Dare to Heal with Spiritual Power, gives the reader many skillful and interesting ways to go beyond judgment of our circumstances and see with new eyes the power of redemption. It helps us to connect with our Divine inheritance to lessen fear and suffering, and be successful in healing our souls and the World.

Burton Bialik, Ph.D.
Psychotherapist

"I Dare to Heal with Spiritual Power" is a profound study of how spiritual tools can make a major impact on not only people who are in pain but also to prevent that suffering as well. Joel Vorensky, taking from his own personal experiences, teaches us how to reach into our own souls and extract those unique powers that can help us to become well. More and more healing practitioners are realizing the power of the spirit in the process of wellness. Prayer is an excellent example that has been proven effective even in scientific studies. Joel Vorensky's new book is a welcome new addition to this field.

Rabbi Moishe Leider
Chabad Center of University City
San Diego, California

CONTENTS

HUMAN QUEST

It is the innate right, evolutionary inevitable, and if necessary, the creative mission of human nature that humankind will come to know inner spiritual peace, harmony, and happiness.

They will come to open their hearts together in a compassionate way, come to learn to create and to share an emotionally safe and trusting space, and come to benefit from attentive listening (both to the message of thought and emotion which is being communicated) in the present moment, to, for, and with each other!

So that humankind together will create a consciousness raising space, where they can effectively share in a heartfelt, loving way their transformational process—an enabling process, to process humankind's profoundest disordered emotions.

Those emotions reflective of vulnerabilities, insecurities, and inadequacies, and thereby, humankind will learn to better accept each other and acknowledge no inner separation.

There is no inner separation of atom, of molecule, of substance of the self.

And we only come to experience the presence of spiritual inner wholeness **and dare to heal with spiritual power.**

The spiritual power that lies within the inner emotional frontiers of the self can be awaken.

And it is within the rainbows of those colorful nuances that we find the shadows, the darkness, and the black holes of inner consciousness. It is here where we awaken both the suppressed and repressed feelings reflective of those emotions.

And in awakening that inner consciousness we come to achieve our purpose of personal growth and healing through spiritual power. It is then that humankind will come to know and share together its birthright to the divine eternal light.

PRELUDE

This is our second journey together. I started on my spiritual journey in 1968 and this book continues insights and experiences that I have accumulated since the publication in 2001 of *I Dare to Heal with Compassionate Love*. This journey will lead us in the steps to and of personal spiritual power and enlightenment. There are definitive steps that need to be taken before we experience liberation from the shadow, darkness, and black holes in our lives. Shadow and darkness are reflective of those inner energies that do not serve our well-being.

This book contains a myriad of methods to enhance and encourage our personal growth, healing, and spiritual power. We can choose to embark upon our spiritual path by choosing a method that best suits our well-being. We choose the method and tools that best resonate with us.

There are some methods/tools that may seem unusual. I ask only that we be open minded and consider them. They are methods/tools that at some point in one's life may become useful. In addition, the book contains stories, insights, and discusses issues.

We bring our liberated energy into the wide world and express it through our personal power for our own and others' well-being and growth. I will be including chapters about how to heal traumas associated with experiences of the San Diego, California, firestorm of October 2003, other firestorms in the state of California and elsewhere, the September 11, 2001, World Trade Center destruction, the Pentagon terrorist attacks, and handling stresses associated with the war in Iraq, the spiritual journeys to Teotihuacan,

Mexico, known as the "Valley of the Gods" and experiences in the
state of Queretero, Mexico.

I will review methods that we can use to achieve personal growth
and heal from emotional trauma/shock. Peer cocounseling is one
method that was established in 1950 and has a documented history
of successes in addressing both emotional and physical impacts of
the dips, bumps, potholes, and craters in our lives. I wrote about
peer cocounseling and its benefits in chapter 3.

I visited the World Trade Center December of 2001 when I was
interviewed by a facilitator of a New York City radio station. There
will be a discussion of additional insights, issues and sharing
additional stories from my and others' experiences. These insights
include emotional "frozen needs." I use and describe the significance
of the "pyramid" of spiritual essence to describe the essential
elements for the personal growth of a human being. We gradually
learn that our personal growth leads to the self-realization that we
are divine.

There will be more music from devotional singing, examples of
spiritual support groups, and metaphysical spiritual book
discussion groups. There will be music by Malaya Rider, Michael
Stillwater, Steve Ducey, Cass Smith, and others. The lyrics are
truly brilliant, and I encourage all to check out their CDs. There
will be a discussion of denial, detachment, the pivotal emotion
fear, the significance of the book cover, victimization, and learning
humility. This book has information that offers hope to many who
have given up because of their emotional ups and downs or shock
of overwhelming emotional experiences.

There are methods that we can invoke to heal from emotional
shock/trauma. They help us to restore aspects of ourselves where
painful emotion has been harbored. The methods can help us find
our spiritual power and enlighten ourselves; become more conscious,
learn to respond more and react less in situations and circumstances

that are beyond and within our control; grow in our self-esteem, character; enhance our humanness; and move toward wholeness once again.

The first book *I Dare to Heal with Compassionate Love* had positive impact on readers. Comments from readers included "It's real" and "It's given me hope." I will elaborate more on the knowledge obtained from healing methods used to negotiate the feelings reflective of emotions. The information is significant to the individual seeking personal growth and spiritual evolution.

I will be writing on a variety of insights, stories, methods, and tools that hopefully will reveal alternatives to readers and how they can negotiate the issues that plague them. The subject of spiritual power and the specific steps when practiced can create authentic transformation of character. I speak about the ten components of the self. I have clearly laid out the ten components of the self and how the emotional component is pivotal in bringing about the fundamental transformation of our being, of our character, and of our life.

What is the significance of our five emotions? The emotions consist of anger, sadness, fear, joy, and love. How do the five emotions mirror our issues, reflect our unhealthy behaviors in the wide world, and depict our tensions caused by damage to our emotional bodies? How are anger, sadness, and fear anchored in frozen needs? How do these frozen needs persist in impacting our rigid behaviors? As always the darkness and shadows we harbor in our collective unconscious can interfere, transform, and paralyze us. They can prevent us from self-realization and cause us endless procrastination and result in putting our lives on hold. It is our choice to become unstuck, but we must have the tools to focus effectively and efficiently on our emotions and those feelings associated with our issues. I will be addressing specific steps so people can use methods and tools that resonate with themselves so they can experience and realize more of their spiritual power. We learn to permeate and surmount individual limitations and maintain a psychological state of faith.

During the past year I've had the privilege to teach English to speakers of other languages and geography at an adult day health care center. The experience of connecting with this group of individuals who are physically, emotionally, and/or cognitively challenged has been exhilarating. The challenge was to be there for them in a creative, loving, passionate, compassionate way. The challenge was to connect with their spiritual essence in order to motivate and energize them. I functioned as a teacher to help them help themselves to nourish their souls with the joy of learning. Theirs is a story of frustration, survival, and hope. Their story is one of human beings' learning to cope with their illness, of daily survival, of gratitude, zest, cooperative interdependence, and joy. Tapping into their strengths by transcending vulnerabilities is also a significant component of their story. I'll be creating a picture of the classroom and the students who participated.

CHAPTER 1

The Pyramid

Definitive Steps to Spiritual Power and Enlightenment

The Introduction of the Pyramid

Humankind is very much a reflection of the structure of a pyramid. We have the mental, emotional, social, physical—heart, soul, and spirit—and at our apex is our spiritual quality, our essence.

We have many facets of ourselves. We have emotional depths, degrees, and dimensions of our mental, emotional bodies. We also have our frozen needs that emanate from our primary and secondary ones.

The Chakras: There are different perspectives of the chakras. There are basically seven chakras.

First and Root Chakra: survival and security

Second Chakra: sexuality, pleasure, primal creativity, sensuality, what arouses passion

Third Chakra: emotions, feel it in my gut

Fourth (Heart) Chakra: love, heartfelt love, self-esteem.

Fifth (throat) Chakra: expression of the state of the first four chakras: expression of security, creativity, emotions, what stirs love

Sixth Chakra: third eye-intuition insight, gestalts of awareness, perception; ability to provide insight into the first four chakras and modify the fifth chakra's expression

Seventh Chakra: gateway to the spiritual realm and to the higher chakras.

I Define Spiritual Power and Enlightenment

The crown chakra is the ultimate in wisdom and spiritual will. It is the dynamics of spiritual perfection through inner contemplation and universal consciousness and spiritual attainment. It is to instruct, to inform to give spiritual insight to, and to illuminate. It's in learning the essence of surrender and release and all of their manifestations that we journey toward more of our selves. We come in greater connection to and in the presence of the divine spark. All humankind can learn to stay connected to that divine spark with greater depth, degree, and emotional dimension.

I've used many methods to obtain spiritual power and spiritual enlightenment. These have included primordial sound, the original sound at birth, primal sound, the sound emanating from the so-called spleen chakra, and the conscious integrated healing transformational circular breath. Peer cocounseling has also been instrumental in my connecting with the essence of spiritual power and enlightenment. These are some of the methods that have opened the door to allowing and permitting me to successfully negotiate, surrender, and release the suppressed and repressed feelings.

Journey into the Valley of the Gods

Teotihuacan, Mexico

I visited the "Valley of the Gods," the spiritual city of Teotihuacan, Mexico, on the summer of 2003. The Valley of the Gods is located approximately forty-five minutes from Mexico City. The bus station in Mexico City Terminal Central de Autobuses del Norte is always a very busy place. I could feel the watchful eyes of security as I waited for the bus to the Valley of the Gods. Mexico City has an unfortunate reputation of being unsafe and a haven for theft.

The bus station is always filled with people on their way to somewhere. The bus station is packed with a variety of shops where you could satisfy a variety of needs. The taxis just outside the station are continuously waved to move on by the police and employees. The noise is constant along with many people seated and waiting for their bus to make its departure. Mexico City is one of the most populated cities in the world.

The bus passes poverty-stricken suburbs on its way to the "City of the Gods." The poverty-stricken areas produce a breeding ground for runaway children and streetwise thieves. The bus was filled to capacity without a seat vacant. I wondered whether it was faith that I sat next to a Mexican man whose name also happened to be Joel.

The landscape turned to the color of green, and the rain continued to pour down. Green is a common color in the country of Mexico.

There are nuances of green that transcend and transform the countryside. The nuances of green reflect the changing landscape as the bus proceeded to its destination.

I arrived at the entrance to the City of the Gods and walked to the entrance of Teotihuacan.
It did not take long before I felt a sense of spiritual coldness to the city. I inquired about its history and was told that people practiced human sacrifice. Could it be that I intuitively felt a spiritual coldness because of this reason?

Later, in San Diego I spoke about my sensation before a group of Mexican adult students who seemed to acknowledge a similar sensation that they had experienced at the City of the Gods. The encouragement quickly came from them to visit more appropriate ruins of Mesoamerica.

The city is said to have been built around one hundred years before the birth of Christ. It was said to be the home of a variety of civilizations. The original creator of Teotihuacan is shrouded in mystery. The Olmeca culture was dominant in Mexico prior to and at the creation of the City of the Gods. The last culture was the renowned culture of the Aztecs.

The City of the Gods is huge. It was once the center of culture, religion, agriculture, technological inventions, and said to be the sixth-largest city in the world with 125,000 inhabitants at the apex of its influence in Mesoamerica. The four principal locations of the city of Teotihuacan are the Avenue of the Dead, the Pyramid of the Sun, the Pyramid of the Moon, and the Feathered Serpent Pyramid. I can speculate that the spiritual peoples who created the pyramids created them as a reflection or model of their own need, want, and desire for spiritual essence and unity of self. The unity is a definition of yoga or the integration and joining of the sun and the moon. The concept is a union of the Pyramid of the Sun and the Pyramid of the Moon. I believe the ancient cultures who resided in this valley had an intuitive insight about personal growth and its connection with a divinity within and without.

The significance of spirituality as it reflects the shape of the pyramid is striking to me. I think of the four or five levels of the pyramids. They can be portrayed as symbols reflective of human qualities depicted in the pyramid constructed above. The apex of the pyramid is symbolic of our spiritual essence.

I speculate that the base of the pyramid represents our primary, secondary, and most importantly, our frozen needs. It is the root of profound energy contained in unfulfilled emotional needs. These unfulfilled needs mirror feelings and tensions throughout our lifetime. I can speculate from my experiences that this is a key component in our spiritual growth and goal of reaching the apex of our individual pyramid. The ultimate goal is that of unity and wholeness.

The other levels are also of significance of course and function as important components in our spiritual growth. I can speculate that the apex of the pyramid is a point where profound energy from thunder and lightning can be absorbed and integrated into the structure. It was appropriate that the spiritual center was constructed in the valley with a dominant view of the surrounding hills.

The pyramid is truly a facsimile of us. The apex of the pyramid can function as a conductor of profound power from lightning and thunder. It is both a primordial and primal power that can lead to great emotional surrenders and release and facilitate profound shifts within, bring about transformation and powerful inner connection and outer connection to our divinity.

I can speculate that the "Plumed Serpent Pyramid" is a representation of the seven coiled energies of the chakras. The plumed serpents essentially are the chakras. The peoples who constructed the series of the pyramids had great insight and understanding of humankind's goal of spiritual essence and the blocked energy of unfulfilled needs; its tension; physical, emotional hurts and traumas that inhibit and block humankind from seeing its way clear to spiritual essence and the apex of humankind's own purity, connection with the divine.

Points to Ponder:

Are you aware of the significance of the coils of energy known as the "chakras"?

Have you ever traveled to ancient ruins and had consciousness-raising experiences about your own personal growth?

Are you aware of any improvements that can be made in your mental, emotional, spiritual, social, and physical aspects of your life?

Do you have activities that contribute to your well-being and personal growth?

CHAPTER 2

Embers of October

The Catastrophic Experience
San Diego, California
Firestorm of 2003

We all have our secrets, but we can never hide those secrets from spirit. We can only open our minds, our hearts, our souls and permit and allow redemption and forgiveness. And by acting so, we experience the divine connection and protection within and without. As Psalm 23 states "Even though I walk through the valley of the shadow of death, I will fear no evil, for you are with me; your rod and your staff, they comfort me" (Psalm 23, A Psalm of David).

There were many homes destroyed during the firestorm, and yet some residences within the devastating destruction were spared. It may have been a reflection of spiritual deliverance. I believe the spiritual essence spared and protected selected homes. I believe that homes saved and homes destroyed represented messages from spiritual essence.

The firestorm showered dust, smoke, ash, sot, dirt, and the terrifying embers in gusty Santa Ana winds around San Diego County. Seventeen lives, two thousand four hundred homes, and half a million acres have been lost or damaged. Lives were lost because some people didn't heed the orders of the county officers to evacuate their homes. Some people left their homes too late and were caught in the firestorm. The firestorm has been so-called frightening and unsettling for many people. There had been many people who have been evacuated. Many of the freeways had been shut down.

I was unsettled and frightened as well by the closeness of the fire to my home. I needed to work through the feelings of my fear and alarm! People were asked to evacuate their residences just three miles from my location. I prepared by packing my important papers into my car. I worked with my own fear using both primal and primordial sound. How wonderfully freeing it is to transform fear into faith.

The air where I live had been very poor, and I had suffered because of my respiratory asthma. I tried to purchase an air filter, but stores claimed they were sold out. I had evacuated the valley where I lived for three nights and stayed with three different friends on the coast. The ocean air was refreshing.

The air seemed better in the valley today after three days of surreal nuances from daylight to darkness. The fires and the winds continued in the mountains.

The fire in the mountains brought the ash, sot, dust, dirt, and the danger of flame embers here into the valley. I am a teacher, but the school districts were closed so there was no work. People evacuated three miles from me, but I believe they returned to their residences.

I had trouble with my car, and I made the repair. I didn't want to have auto problems if and when I needed to immediately evacuate.

The children have become disoriented. School districts have been closed and the children's routine had been disrupted. The younger children just didn't understand what was happening in the world. The younger children needed to be reassured by their parents.

A commentator who was normally on radio stayed at home. He called his radio show and spoke with his replacement and reported on the fire in his area. He claimed that the fire from his point of view was "mildly entertaining" while he was observing the flames.

Many had no electricity in San Diego County and this included the radio commentator. He wasn't entertained by the lack of electricity and living by candlelight in his residence.

People were actually entertaining themselves by driving to those areas of the county that had been devastated by the fire and were taking photographs of the homes that had been burned down to a chimney. One man claimed that the sound of the fire was magical.

The following are quotes from comments by individuals on TV and radio:

"The fire had jumped the freeway," claimed one call-in commentator.

The Viejas Indian Reservation Casino had been threatened, but through the hard, tireless work of the firefighters it was saved.

Animals were impacted greatly. Horses were released to run wild. Some locations were taking animals. Some private ranches were taking horses. Rodeo grounds were taking animals. Animals died, and some were evacuated.

The firefighters were outgunned by every turn but had worked tirelessly and had saved many homes.

San Diego Gas and Electric claimed transformers and power poles had melted and it will take three days for power to return in certain areas. SDG&E had to cut off the gas from residences because of the firestorm.

A woman claimed she videotaped a propane tank that had blown up and a building that was immersed in flames.

Driving to his destination on a main freeway, a county councilman claimed seeing autos melt in driveways.

"It's was an eerie sight!"

"When will the mail delivery resume?" asked one radio call-in person.

"I guess it looks like a war zone, it's all bombed out!"
"Give us a call. Our phone number here is 222-234-3456. Call in and let us hear what your experience is," said the radio talk show host.

If you smell and see smoke, if it's uncomfortable, the response should be to get out!

None of the buildings at Deer Creek Meadows had been burned down, but on the Heights one or two houses had been destroyed!

In the Crest area of San Diego County most of the homes were gone.

In the Scripps area there was total devastation!

"It's hard to believe. It's just hard to believe that the firestorm came this far."

"It's been difficult to get to the fires because of the rocky terrain."

A new highway closure—Old Highway 80—at Flinn Springs.

Comments from the October 28, 2003 Tragedy

"We saw at least twenty homes burned on one street." People's hopes and dreams gone in one blaze.
It is nuances of total grief, anger, and fear.

"I walked out of a meditation service and the scene was like a science-fiction movie. Everyone was wearing a protective mask. The sun was like a ball of red. Like the sun it was a reflection of the impermanence of all things."

"It was like the end of all time."

"We are always caught with our pants down."

"We have to 'John Wayne' it."

"We need a rapid reaction force."

"If there is smoke, there is fire."

"I wonder how many people were ill prepared for this kind of situation."

"There are probably high-priced lawyers who are now debating how our insurance companies can get out of taking responsibility for reimbursing their insureds."

"It's just an eerie site."

"I saw the flames, and they were horrible, they were horrible."

"Some people are absolutely devastated by the loss of their homes."

"If nothing else you are in shock."

"Most people will probably stay and rebuild.
We're all neighbors, we will all stay, and rebuild.
We were one of the lucky ones. Our house was saved yesterday."

"It's been tough; we are still without power here."

"There is basically one way up here and only one way down. It's scary."

"The fire department is spread thin."

"You get to know strangers and get to know your friends better."

Comment from a pilot: "The height of the fire is approximately five hundred feet; it's both surreal and humbling."

"We are seeing a fire season that no one can ever remember."

The wind has died down in an eerie, surreal way.

"When I hear the politicians pointing their fingers at other politicians regarding not taking responsibilities for supplying the assets in responding to the fire I cannot help but to think the accusations are irresponsible."
"The fire is threatening to jump the freeway."

"It's a risk we all take as firefighters, and sometimes we pay the highest price."

October 29, 2003

"I saw the house burn down in real time."

"A beautiful light has been turned off, and I don't know how we will get on without her." (Speaking of a lost loved one to the firestorm).

"The palm tree on the adjacent property exploded and caused the fire destruction of our rear door."

"We're really blessed with our own situation because we know some people lost everything."

"When they say leave, 'leave.'"
"There is denial."

"Yesterday, cars were driving with there lights on, there was ash and soot everywhere, and today I can see blue skies."

"This fire is dynamic—it's unforgiving, and it's tragic."

"This fire is being called the beast."

"The winds were moving at about thirty-five mph."

"Country folk were impacted. City folk were impacted."

"It's amazing! Poor people, rich people—all were impacted."
"Lost Pets. Phone number: 619-236-4250"
"We've survived two nights of hell. I've seen one-hundred-foot flames."

"The winds today have been a real problem. They've been gusty today up to thirty-five mph and up to fifty mph."

"We received an amber alert." The amber alerts is the alert to prepare to evacuate.

"My sister returned to her house and everything was burned down except there was an angel figurine left untouched above the fireplace."

"They've saved a lot of my neighbors' homes in the canyon, and I've lost everything."

"I lost my husband to cancer several months ago. I lost my house in the 'firestorm.' My daughter was sifting through the rubble of our house. There was nothing left except we found my husband's wedding ring."

October 30, 2003

"Presently, there is a hundred-mile fire line where we are fighting the fire."

"I have never seen anything like this in my firefighting history."

"Everywhere, everywhere I look, it's burned."

"It's such a sickening feeling to watch the fire and know that so many people have been in the storm's path."
"They didn't have a chance."

"It's the devastation that produces the most remarkable images."
"Some places have been preserved."

"There are a total of three hundred twenty-eight thousand acres burned in San Diego County and one firefighter dead."

The attitude of the firefighter: Let's save this house, and let's save the next one.

"I'm walking up and down, and they don't let me back to my house."

"When the propane tanks blew up in front of us, we hit the deck. We just stuck through it."

October 31, 2003

"Today the rains came. The rains came with a sense of relief. We all needed it to rain to give us a sense of relief."

"The effects of the firestorm and the lives it has impacted, the shadow, the darkness, the hurt, and the trauma it has produced will cause lasting impact for many of us. It's important to remember that where there is darkness and trauma, bright stars are present. It's my hope that those who have been impacted will reach out and touch those stars within. It's my hope that those people, like me, will expand the sparkling, blinking stars into more light! For to stay in the shadow, the darkness, the denial is just not a choice nor is it an option, we must continue to reach out for more support and light!

Many people are walking around in shock and are not conscious of those feelings!"

"Every bit of emotional counseling shall be available!"

"The death toll stands today at sixteen deaths, two thousand homes damaged and destroyed, and three quarters of a billion dollars in loss."

"If this weather holds we can contain the firestorm by Sunday."

"There is an overcast cloudy sky today, and on the corner of Friars Road and Riverdale there is an eight-by-twelve-feet sign. In big black and red letters it states: We restore smoke-damaged clothing, phone 619-282-1763."

News Reporters' Comments:

"It's heartbreaking to see all the devastation today."

"We have not been exposed to this devastation before."

"What is you reaction to what you have seen?"
    "It's heartbreaking."
    "The biggest fire is here."
    "This struck me as the biggest 'dateline'"
    "Right here is the heart of the story."

"He was in tears."

"The firestorm is messing with the mail. If you are not getting your mail, please pick it up at your local office."

"We're seeing people driving down the street and seeing people's jaws dropping as they discover their homes that have been devastated."

"Mandatory evacuations had been ordered for the unincorporated areas of the county for Descanso."

"It's a wonder how sheer terror can give way to tedium."

"It's very foggy out there; it's very smoky out there; and it's very dangerous."

"There's a long ring of fire that stretchers twenty-five to thirty miles."

"It's like David going up against Goliath."

"There are a dozen homes below me that are burning in flames."

"If you are scared and twenty to thirty miles from where the fire had been reported to be 'just get out.'"

"We just got two confirmations that three firefighters have lost their lives in the fires. We have confirmed one firefighter dead, one severely injured, and two others injured."

"This is an advisory. The sheriff's department is asking residents of Ramona to be prepared to get out."

"It was like a big tornado came up, the sky was gray and was like the end of the world."

"It's a major fear that the fire will crest a ridge and jump a highway."

"The winds kept on playing tricks. The smoke is getting thicker, the winds are coming."

"The wind is inhibiting our control efforts."

"Watching fire spread can be a paralyzing image if this was your house and these are your bushes."

"We've had four firefighters that were overcome by flames. We do have a fatality and three injured."

"It's not the big ugly scene we've seen a few days ago."

"A few hours ago the winds were working with the firefighters, but now they are beginning to change."

"Some homes can be saved, but others are left to the fire's wrath."

"These conditions are absurd." (Referring to fifty mph winds in the mountains.)

Newspaper Headlines:

Raging "Cedar Fire" now biggest blaze in county history.

Smoky air causes run on masks and visits to hospitals.

New crews on way to join firefight.

A statue of the Virgin Mary stood in front of a destroyed house on Harbison Canyon Road yesterday.

It's house-to-house combat as aid awaited.

Pine trees went up in a roar leaving these fire skeletons.

Off-road enthusiasts and environmentalists are asking people to
stay off burned land so it can *heal.*

Headlines regarding firefighters:

Some firefighters are being taken off the lines.

They are hungry, they are tired, and they are being taken off the
fire lines.

They hadn't eaten since yesterday.

Every house on this block has been burnt down.

There are five firefighters who have lost their homes fighting fires
for others in order to save their residences.

Comments from the Government:

"President Bush has declared San Diego County a 'Disaster Area.'"

"We do know these people were killed in their vehicles when they
were evacuating the area."

"They have Red Cross aid. They have disaster aid."

"We're doing all we can to put the fires out and put their [people's]
lives in order."

"Some conditions have improved with the decrease in the winds
offshore."

"I believe the governor's word."

"The government has reassured us."

"The numbers associated with this firestorm are staggering."

"Obey all orders if the order of evacuation comes."

"We are going to get through this."

"Our response to this situation has been courageous."

"This situation has been dangerous to infants, children, and those with respiratory diseases like asthma."

"We have received an advisory from the water district: disinfect your drinking water in the affected areas."

"We have lost cell phone towers; we have lost landline connects."

"If you don't belong in the affected areas, don't go there."

"We will begin a process of providing aid to the city and county of San Diego after meeting with the Undersecretary of FEMA [Federal Emergency Management Agency]."
"We're trying to get every asset we can onto this fire."

"We are then going to review everything we can to get through the bureaucracy."

"The fire's spread rate has been six thousand acres per area; we have never seen this speed rate of a fire spread in my past experience."

Said to reporters by a fire chief: "I think you need to focus on the good and stop focusing on the bad."

"I don't think there have been significant delays."
"The support has been overwhelming."

"The decision was made that the use of federal aircraft pilots would be too dangerous. It would be too dangerous flying into the stricken areas because of the density of the smoke and the wind currents."

"We wanted to cut down the unwanted trees, but it was the environmentalists that got in the way."

"I want to thank the overwhelming support received from the community here in San Diego County."

"I can't believe everybody got out of their houses, I'm afraid we'll be finding more bodies."

"There have been incredible losses."

"I've seen moms and dads weeping."

"I'm seeing charred, smoldering remains."

"I've seen children, moms, and dads looking through rubble."

"We need to do everything we can to get the bureaucracy out of the way and get the rebuilding process on the way."

"I don't think people realize the wall of flame and heat that the firefighters were up against."

"This wall of flame set off fires in so many different places at one time."

"The good news is that the town of Julian still stands."

"We're not out of this yet."

"The bad news is that the town of Cuyamaca is gone."

County Council Persons' Comments:

"I'm going through every community in the district and have my staffs listen to people."

"I'm still hearing a lot of emotion."

"I know the emotion is getting in the way, please be specific about your needs. If you need vouchers, if you need a place to stay, if you need clothes, we'll be providing specific needs."

"It was a tremendous fear, and it looks like the worst case scenario has materialized."

"This is a definite war zone here."

"We thought there would be help from the weather, but it's not going to happen."

"There are two hundred fifty thousand acres burning in San Diego County."

"This is the largest fire ever in the state of California."

"We have built a city here to fight this war."

"I'll do all I can to get all the money I can for the victims of the fire."

"We've survived before, and we'll survive again. We will rise from the ashes once again."

"We have no power, we have no electricity."

"The fire spread so fast no one could believe it."

November 30:

The mayor: "This is a sad day for San Diego but a proud day for the city. Lives have been saved!"

Governor's Schwarzenegger inaugural speech included these comments in the month of November.

"As Californians, we will mourn together, we will fight together, we will rebuild together."

Weather Reporters' Comments:

"The air quality is still unhealthy."
"The rains came today, it was godsent!"

Psychiatrist's comments:

"Acknowledge the grief deeply. Anger is the first emotion that comes up in these situations. The anger gives way to sadness and grief. Express both grief and gratitude. Often it can impact your relationships. Some people are quiet. Some are very expressive. Give space to express feelings. Ask what you are going through. Acknowledge that it's tough. Don't promise that everything is going to be all right. Accept the reality now."

The Firestorm Trauma

The Aftermath

Karen drove through the town of Ramona and claimed that the twigs and power lines were burnt, and the earth looked like a graveyard.

Jim sold tee shirts for the benefit of the police and firefighters who could not obtain aid from the Red Cross and who have lost their homes fighting to save the homes of others.

The bilingual kindergarten contained eighteen children who were present that day. The location of the school is in the Otay District where the firestorm had occurred just a week ago. I wonder whether or not the children had spoken about their feelings regarding the fire. I wonder whether or not anyone had bothered to ask them what they saw or what they heard. Whether or not they had experienced any sadness, anger, or fear.

I asked all eighteen kids in the class. and all the kids responded that they all had felt sadness and fear about the firestorm. Jane felt sad because she saw her mom struggle with the smoke. Martha felt afraid because she had to put on a mask that prevented the dust, soot, dirt, smoke, and ash from entering her lungs. Jose felt afraid because he had to evacuate his home suddenly. Tom felt angry that he had to leave his friends in the neighborhood. Jim felt afraid because he saw the firestorm on TV, and he heard that it was coming to his home.

A.J. saw the fire from his bedroom window. His dad brought the firestorm to A.J.'s attention. A.J. expressed his fear and was still traumatized by seeing the raging fire through the transparency of the glass. The children needed to speak about their feelings. They needed someone to listen with empathy and to acknowledge their emotions. I listened to the children express their feelings in both the English and Spanish language. I gave them an opportunity and created a safe space for them to speak about their individual experiences.

We avoid speaking about our feelings. We avoid listening to each others experience and avoid asking about our emotional experience. The emotional body seldom ever gets heard and therefore acknowledged. The pain just accumulates in the body and creates emotional and physical disease.

There is a chronic lack of acknowledgment by teachers, administrators, and parents of the emotions of children and each other. There just never seems to be enough time to engage each other in attentive listening. There seems to be an embarrassment created by the socialization process that prevents acknowledgement of our emotional body.

Conscious teachers, administrators, and parents maintain an awareness of what and how traumatic situations and circumstances impact themselves and their children. The emotional education is as important as math, English, social studies, and science. It needs to be taught in the schools. It needs to be a focus in curriculum. Parents need to request and demand it. Students need to request and demand it of their parents. Students need to become aware of their emotional needs to express their hurt and traumatizing experiences. The system must stop ignoring the reality of the impact of emotional hurt and trauma upon education. It soon becomes an inhibiting factor for children in the learning process.

I taught a fourth-grade class and spoke about the five feelings common to all of us—sadness, anger, fear, joy, and love." I asked them about the "firestorm" and what they heard, what they saw, and what they felt?

There were twenty-eight children in the class and about ten children volunteered to express their thoughts and feelings. The consensus was that the children all felt a sense of sadness and fear. These feelings were also true of a group of students in a bilingual first-grade class as well.

There still needs to be an ongoing effort from adults to ask children their feelings and a willingness to be sensitive to and listen to the thoughts and feelings of the children.

Points to Ponder:

Have you ever experienced a major disaster in your environment? Have you ever dared to explore the feelings within yourself subsequent to your environmental disaster experience?

Are you willing to aid others in their exploration of their feelings by listening to them?

In memory of fireman Steven Rucker from Novato, California.

CHAPTER 3

The Door Openers
A Significant Door Opener

Right Action

Using right processes leads to healthy thinking. Right thinking leads to healthy feeling. Right feeling leads to healthy intention. Right intention leads to healthy action. Right action leads to productive results which leads to healthy and right character.

Peer Cocounseling

There is a great deal of documentation on the benefits of peer cocounseling that dates back over forty years. It's a simple but dynamic and powerful process. Peer cocounseling is a process that involves a series of steps. The individuals agree to share a period of time and take turns listening to new and good, identification (who they remind each other of), minor and major upsets; tell their stories; and share looking-forward techniques.

I like the rule of no socializing and no sexual involvement in the method. The policy of "no sexual involvement" contradicts powerfully the tendency to fulfill frozen chronic needs that individuals harbor in their collected unconscious.

I like the power of the compassionate intimacy that can evolve in a cocounseling peer relationship. Nonsexual compassionate intimacy is a catalyst that facilitates peer counselors to surrender/release and discharge their feelings. It's a loving process that dynamically unfolds for both counselors as their relationship evolves, and both are productive in their personal growth.

I like the attributes of cocounseling. The client is in charge of his process at all times. I like the class model where one can meet other cocounselors and get to know each other so trust can develop among the participants. I like the flexibility of participating in a so-called session by taking turns to counsel a client by telephone or in person.

There are two people who work together whose focus is a sharing of attentive attention. They take turns giving and receiving aware attention. They do not advise, share their experience, gossip, have an agenda with each other, judge, interfere with what is said to each other, become friends, socialize, but work together in and with an understanding of confidentiality. The goal is to create a safe space where both individuals can express freely in an animated tone of voice what they need or want to express. The goal is to create a safe space where both individuals can free themselves from hurt and traumatizing experiences. People can choose to gradually learn to express and negotiate both suppressed and repressed feelings. The partners can work on minor or major upsets, feelings associated with frozen unfulfilled needs, and other issues from the past as well as the present.

We learn and experience emotional discharge in the peer cocounseling method. Our socialization process inhibits the manifestations of emotional surrender and release. We lose the natural, innate ability to "let go" at a very early age. We lose the natural, innate ability to have that "good cry." We became sold on the effectiveness of the process after a successful experience of emotional discharge. Classes can be taken to relearn the manifestations and profound benefits of emotional discharge, surrender, and release.

We can derive clarity of thought through the discharge of disordered feelings reflective of emotions. We learn through emotional discharge that we can feel better and make more rational decisions and make better rational choices in our lives. We can make mistakes in our decisions, and our decisions can be reversible with more information dependent upon situation or circumstance.

Peer cocounseling is an excellent method/tool to address many emotionally upsetting experiences such as issues of fear, anxiety, sadness, depression, irritation, and anger.

We learn that surrendering and releasing our feelings is a positive and healthy process. It is here where we learn to master the surrender and release of nuances of the shadow and dark feelings and address unfulfilled tensions emanating from frozen needs.

It is here where we learn the depth, degree, and emotional dimensions of unproductive feelings within our emotional body. Feelings are reflective of fear, sadness, and anger. It is through this method where we learn how to address in a focused, effective, and efficient way feelings in the collective conscious and unconscious.

Because we choose to address our emotions through this process, we create a bridge to our spiritual body and learn to deepen our spiritual experience within. It then creates a trusting, nurturing space where we and our peer counselors learn to be there for each other in an empathetic, compassionate, attentive manner for each others' personal power and enlightenment.

We learn through peer counseling to tune into when someone isn't in their personal power. We listen to many clients and become attuned to when they aren't resonating from themselves but resonating from their emotional hurts and/or traumas. We develop the ability to counsel people when we perceptively pick up the dissonance in their voices and/or body language. It's a learning process used to differentiate the person from their pattern of distress.

We learn to listen without judging and thereby develop the sensitivity to differentiate between the dissonance in thought, feeling, and authentic thought connected to feeling. The dissonance of thought and feeling reflects the emotional hurt and trauma. We learn to see beyond the dissonance of thoughts and feelings and make suggestions to support human reemergence from distress. It is in this way that we have also learned to differentiate the person from the destructive human distresses, the patterns that cause unhealthy, self-defeating, and destructive behavior.

The impact of peer counseling helps us to develop empathy and compassion because of our experience of nonjudgmental listening. Our training and practice then enable us to see beyond the thoughts and feelings of the client to his spiritual essence.

The empathy and compassion is the bridge to spiritual healing. The spiritual space opens the door for an inner and outer connection with spirit. The creation of a spiritual connection allows for a spiritual voice to be heard by the individual. We can find answers to our burdens and questions when we create this emotional empathetic space. We create harmony and peace within!

We learn to take the time to be there and create a cognitive and emotional space to be fully present when we listen. We take the time to be there in an empathetic and compassionate way as well.

The capacity for having enough time and space for listening is essential in the healing, evolution, and expansion of ourselves. In this way we can be fully present to listen to each other. This is a quality we develop as peer cocounselors.

Peer cocounseling methods are not enough. It is the reason why I wrote about the significance of the primal and primordial sounds. The sounds are significant in permeating chronic emotional distress, frozen chronic needs, and severe trauma.

Peer counseling enables us to develop the self-confidence and trust to use the "integrated, circular, connected, divine, transformational, healing breath" and the primal and primordial sound" to surrender and release any and all suppressed and repressed feelings at any depth, degree, intensity, density, and emotional dimension within our emotional body. We achieve this gradually in time.

When the cocounselors develop enough experience, both suppressed and repressed feelings begin to emerge from the depths of their emotional bodies. It's like a balloon that surfaces from within filled with feelings from the collected and uncollected consciousness. Suppressed feelings are those feelings we are aware of and repressed feelings are those feelings that we are unaware of. The feelings are manifested in a variety of natural ways. The animated talking, animated laughing, yawning, tearing, hot and cold sweating, shivering and shaking, scratching, active kidneys, expressing anger, storming, and sadness are common. These manifestations take place when the individual *makes the decision to cross over to surrender and release their emotional tension.* This occurs when there is enough attentive attention present for an individual in present time. Cocounselors describe it as a balance of attention. This takes place when the individual has the will to take charge of his life and "let go and let God in."

When there is enough emotional surrender and release, when the individual has successfully gone into and gone through the *feelings*, and when they have been thoroughly *emoted*, then transformation in behavior is accomplished. The key word here is the word "enough." This is a significant gate to walk or push through. It's a maturing process. I worked with myself from 1967 until 1972 until I was able to pass through this emotional gate. I passed through this door because I decided that I dared to heal with my own spiritual power. We all have to make this decision in order to succeed on our individual journeys.

I learned to effectively and efficiently focus to successfully negotiate emotion over a three-year period. I learned to experience the nuances and learned to become comfortable feeling my feelings. This experience gave me the anchoring, the foundation, the trust, the sense of security to address profounder hurts, traumas, and frozen needs, feel the feelings and learn the surrender and release of those feelings.

Peer cocounseling claims that a human being moves through specific degrees and depths of emotional release as it relates to the distress experience on their way toward healing. The human being moves through steps in the manifestation and surrender of distress. The human being evolves through emotional release and successfully liberates their emotional body from the distress associated with the experience. The patterns begin to fall away as an individual begins to express their feelings.

It is also here where we learn to deepen our cognitive abilities in so-called think-and-listen sessions. They can focus in a cognitive way to reevaluate minor or major upset experiences.

Peer cocounseling is an excellent vehicle to deepen one's cognitive abilities. We can use the attention we are receiving to think through a situation or circumstance. If and when clear thinking is blocked by an emotion, then one can invoke emotional release manifestations until clarity of thought is achieved.

Peer cocounselors belong to a community of counselors. The group activity strengthens individuals in their individual cocounselor relationships. The peer counseling functions well when rules are followed and a willingness of participation by its participants are present.

Giving and Receiving

The most beautiful giving and receiving that two people can extend to each other is the giving and receiving of intimate empathy and compassion that can be experienced in a peer cocounseling relationship. When peer counseling works well, the result is an integration of that part of the self previously enameled in pain energy, and the result is more human authenticity.

We can use animated talking and animated laughing to release feelings from within. We can experience wonderful periods of emotional release through tremendous amounts of divine laughter. We also use a crisp, clear, clean, long, and divine yawn as well to release feelings that are reflective of emotional upsets. I truly feel relaxed after using the divine yawn for a period of thirty minutes to one hour.

I use the word "divine" because it's truly a spiritual experience that restores personal power to my body and helps to raise my awareness about a situation or circumstance. I usually continue the process for a period of thirty minutes to an hour. Cocounselors divide the amount of time decided upon beforehand. We can decide upon ten minutes each. A session of short duration is known as a minisession in co-counseling terminology. Individuals can decide on longer periods of time as well. The time consideration is always left to the individuals who participate in the process. The result of this process for me is either to restore peace, happiness, and harmony within or to expand upon it.

A Shift into Reality

There is a partial shift into reality that takes place when we do our work of release. The shift has the effect to begin transitioning a present or prior stress or distress experience. We experience more energy and life vitality. Once again we work toward enlightenment and to restore our spiritual power. We can also begin to experience a transformation of the self. It is here where we begin the process of the synthesis and integration of the self that occurs when more freed-up vital energy is restored.

The shift can be described as either in part or a complete transformation. One may feel like the "shift" or "shifts" may result in a complete and final shift and a final "right of passage." However, it may be necessary to have many emotional shifts, until a right of passage is achieved.

The negative emotional pattern may be triggered or retriggered again and again. It's the reason why many so-called shifts may be necessary. It's an integration of free-flowing vital energy that eventually returns to the self.

Points to Ponder:

Have you ever had a good, trusted friend who you felt emotionally safe with?

Have you experienced an emotional space where you could in an animated way express your thoughts and feelings?

Have you ever been authentically listened to? How did that feel?

Have you ever had a so-called prayer partner?

How have you felt after someone had been wholly there just for you?

Have you experienced and realized emotional shifts in your life?

CHAPTER 4

The Emotional Nuances

And I will restore to you the years that the locust hath eaten, the cankerworm, and the caterpillar, and the palmerworm, my great army which I sent among you.

—Joel 2:25

There is a tremendous amount of energy contained in anything physical.

—Einstein's Law of Relativity

"We cannot help but to find life's passion within the nuances of emotion."

"We learn to permit and allow ourselves to feel our feelings."

The Key Component to Spiritual Power and Enlightenment

There are endless shadows and darkness that come and prevail in Scandinavia from fall through spring. The spring comes in May, and life begins again to awaken from its sleepy hibernation. The shadows and darkness soon enfold Northern Europe in the fall like they can envelope a human self and cast a spell of depression, anxiety, and hopelessness.

There is a village in Sweden where in 1973 I reconnected and discovered my emotional essence. I had an experience that was life transforming for me. I reconnected with my emotional essence with the support of some very compassionate individuals.

I attended a reevaluation cocounseling workshop over a weekend and connected with a tremendous amount of accumulated tension. For the first time in years, I was able to express my sorrow. I allowed and permitted myself to feel my feelings at every opportunity during a counseling session. The experience was a rebirth for me. In this way I definitively reconnected to my emotional body.

I had been seeking a connection with my stored-up emotions since 1968 without success until that snowy weekend in February 1973. I have met people who have yet rediscovered their emotional essence and have yet began to develop their emotional quotient within. They have become distant from their humanity within. We can discover more of our humanity by experiencing our inner frontiers of emotion.

We spend most of our lives ignoring our emotions and never giving ourselves the opportunity of experiencing fully those emotions that feel painful or as I like to say "energy that doesn't serve us." The tensions build in our body, and we do not acknowledge them or do all that we can to be in denial of them.

Our emotional walls are created. We become more and more disconnected from feeling—our feelings. We all have experienced many people who just seem hollow from the inside out. They just don't seem to have had a "good" cry in years. They just seem to somehow be filled with tension. The tension can lead to a myriad of diseases.

Our inner emotional tone can be seen and felt in the wide world. Our emotional tone can reflect both our behaviors and appearance. It can impact our relationships and our behaviors as well.

We soon begin to realize that the feelings in our emotional body have ranges reflective of the different hurtful experiences. We soon begin to realize our disordered feelings. There is a range of emotion that encompasses anger through rage, fear through terror, and sadness through grief. We learn their nuances, their depths, degrees, dimensions, their emotional densities, and intensities. They reflect the past and present dips, bumps, potholes, and craters in our lives. They are our hurts and traumas.

In a somewhat similar way we can think of our emotions in mathematical linear terms. Linear units are defined as length, width, height, and distance. We can equate these terms with our emotional range, degree, depth, and multiple dimensions.

We can speculate that our dreams are reflective of our emotional ranges. We can have very colorful dreams which are reflective of our emotions and their dimensions. The chief dimensions being emotional time and space. The hurt feeling holds emotional feeling space. The hurt feelings occupy our thoughts. The thoughts take our attention and therefore take emotionally our time. We tend to become preoccupied with our thoughts that are reflective of our hurt feelings. The hurt feelings become reflective of our thoughts which remove and take our attention away from the wide world.

When we surrender and release our hurt feelings in our emotional body, we essentially cleanse our spirit, our soul. We then can experience clarity and insight! This cleansing opens the door for a spiritual connection with the divine. The cleansing creates clean, clear, and crisp spiritual callings and messages from the divine entity.

The Fountain of Youth

We learn that in doing our work to strengthen our emotional quotient we experience a "fountain of youth." We connect with an infinite sense of youthfulness that is clear, crisp, and clean. It can be seen in our face, in our tone, in our smile, in our body language. The miracle of the fountain of youth occurs when one dares to feel one's feelings when one gets hurt. The peace and the bliss flow in, and the energy of pain flow out. The pain energy flows back into a space void of time and divine energy. The pain energy flows back into nothingness. We experience stillness and nothingness within after we adequately surrender and release our pain energy. The disordered feelings of sadness, anger, fear, tensions from old hurts and traumas are expressed, and the results are stillness and tranquility within. It's a breath of inner fresh air that circulates throughout the inner mind, soul, and spirit.

We expand, evolve our divinity. It is a wonder, an enchantment to be filled with inner space filled with divine inner energy. One cannot help but to be in a state of celebration. The state of celebration is a state of consciousness reflective of inner personal power—open heart, mind, and an enlighten soul.

It's important for us to persist in our journey of an inner experience and expression of our feelings. It is in the effective, efficient, focused, and gradual experience of exploring the range of our feelings reflective of our emotions that we experience more of ourselves.

Our feelings include our repressed, unfulfilled frozen needs. This is reflective of our hurts and traumas that we, with determination, can transform into our spiritual power in the wide world.

We must be willing to practice our methods that help us help ourselves. We must be willing to do the necessary work to manifest ourselves. We can learn to do the work effortlessly or with effort. We must do the work on a continual basis. We must develop our methods/tools that resonate with ourselves. We must learn to use our methods/tools that help us help ourselves whenever the circumstances or situations are calling and necessary. This could be during the day and/or at night. If we encounter a situation that wakes us in the middle of the night, then we can choose to immediately use a method to surrender and release feelings whether they be suppressed or repressed. We must respond to the calling of feelings that are surfacing and address our emotions. We can intuitively in an unconscious way know or consciously know this by way of our thoughts.

However we do the work, wherever we do the work—in bed, the car, a telephone booth, in nature—whenever we do the work, whoever we do the work with, there is no getting around from doing it. We cannot cheat, we cannot procrastinate, we cannot make excuses nor ignore the existence of our accumulated baggage nor can we be in denial of it. The mind, the heart, the soul, the body, the emotions, the spirit, the intuition tell us if and when the work is necessary.

We need to be sensitive to the calling of our issues by learning to hear and to listen to our emotions. We need to be alert and open to opportunities that call us to explore our inner frontiers. We always know when we need to do the work because the mind, the body, the heart, the soul, the emotions, the situation, the circumstances will make themselves known to us.

We must be open to listen to what the mind, the body, the emotions, the heart, the soul, the spirit voices communicate with and tell us. We must be open to our experiences. Our inner voices will always call on us. We need to and are called to learn to be open to hear and listen to our inner voices.

If and when circumstances warrant our feeling sad, angry, or fearful then it's time to heal that wound. We just do not wait and allow our feelings to become suppressed to our consciousness or repressed to our repressed collected unconscious. We direct our attention to feeling our feelings and subsequently we learn of and about our liberation. We learn to choose to respond to situations and find it less healthy to react to situations and circumstances.

We learn to capitalize on what we perceive to be tensions triggered or difficult situations of mind, body, and spirit that challenge our personal growth which calls forth our methods/tools to do the necessary personal work. When our minds are running with thoughts that do not stop it usually is an indication that feelings and/or unaware tensions are calling us to address our issues.

We encounter situations and circumstances where old hurts and traumas are triggered. Feelings associated with those tensions fill our emotional body.

We will always know when we have done enough work because we will need to rest and sleep to restore ourselves.

The analogy is with Mother Earth, its crust, her plates/shelves, Earth's mantle and core, and a volcanic eruption. There is a liquid around Earth's core. The liquid is like repressed feelings creating tension for the individual. It is here where magma or tension in the body/mountain builds until there is an eruption or a profound release of feelings/tension.

Everybody has their individual patterns just like every volcano has their unique patterns. The scientist searches for patterns in volcanic magma. The magmalike feelings creates dissonance in a mountain. The feelings are like the magma creating dissonance within us as well. The subterranean heat in a volcano is like the repressed feelings in the collected unconscious of a human being. There is gas and air in a volcano that creates tension with nowhere to go in the volcano itself except to erupt. The feelings resonate within us in the form of tension. We can address their patterns by way of our awareness of, intuition to, and alertness with suppressed and repressed feelings. The feelings can be our tensions associated with our hurts and traumas. When tensions build in the body from feelings after being triggered on a regular or intermittent basis, the feelings need to be surrendered and released. When we hold our feelings within without expressing them they can only harm us.

When the emotional storm comes to and end, we subsequently experience profound silence of peace within. It is just like the volcano. When the lava stops flowing from the volcano there is peace in nature.

We can focus on the throat and the gut or the chakra located in the solar plexus. It is in these two chakras where we experience the "feelings." We begin to get emotional life in our emotional feeling body when we begin to experience those feelings. They are within those parts and/or facets of our emotional selves that make up our shadows, darkness, and black holes.

When we succeed at surrendering and releasing our stored-up tension we have an experience of expansion, evolution, possibly a potential revolution of that part of the self that was formerly occluded in shadow and darkness.

The self as I see it is comprised of ten parts, i.e., mental, emotional, spiritual (when we pray we endow our spirit with the spiritual), physical, social (the community), heart, soul, creative, intuitive. Please refer to the pyramid diagram in chapter 1.

The work that we do, reflective of those methods that resonate with ourselves, brings results of clarity or light to that part of the emotional body where previously there was either conscious or unconscious hurt and trauma. The result is a further integration, synthesis, and liberation of that part of the self that was previously in darkness.

Nature, life, the universe, humankind celebrates this achievement! It can only be described as a fountain of youth, an authentic renewal, a rebirth, a holotropic experience, (toward the whole) an ecstatic experience, a Kundalini experience (an awakening), but above all a human one. It's the greatest exploration of emotional truth and significant in our quest for spiritual enlightenment and spiritual power! As an example, ponder any emotional hurt experienced in relationship. Imagine how you would feel without that issue. Imagine it now!

Emotional Energy Builds Up in the Chakras: We can feel the accumulation of emotional stress in our body and how it harbors in the pelvic, below the navel, below the solar plexus, around the heart (anxiety), in the throat, around the third eye (migraines), and at the crown of the head.

Emotional Strain / Emotional Limitations

It's important to come to know one's emotional reactions and limitations in order to avoid emotional strain. It's important to be sensitive to one's emotional hot buttons. When we are aware and alert about our emotional hot buttons, we can make appropriate adjustments in our thoughts, in moving from our emotional reactions to emotional responses. We act to do this so we can refrain from hurting ourselves.

Governor Howard Dean in the primary elections of 2004 is an excellent example of a candidate who reacted from anxiety because of his defeat in Iowa. Voters became disenchanted with Governor Dean because of his overreaction to his loss. Voters may consider Governor Dean overreacting with dignitaries in the wide world. Such behavior is inappropriate for high office. The key is to learn how to react calmly and patiently but decisively when life situations and circumstances just don't seem to go one's way.

Emotional Rigidities

When we experience too much pain, emotional rigidities can become integrated in us and change our behavior. We respond to new circumstances and situations in patterned and rigid ways. The excessive pain creates the rigidities and only the focused, effective, and efficient surrender and release of the feelings helps to transform and integrate ourselves once again.

I think we have all experienced people whose behaviors have changed because of experiencing too much emotional pain. Our body language transmits our rigidity, and only the surrender of the feelings impacts a transition to a more-flexible intelligence and body language.

If we experience too much grief, rage, or terror, rigid behaviors develop. We can actually feel the rigidity in ourselves when we experience too much grief. It is like an emotional wall is created. We also feel the wall dissipating when we surrender and release the emotion reflective of our feelings from within our emotional body. We then begin to liberate ourselves from the emotional rigidity.

Daydreaming

I have often watched children daydream in the classroom and have asked myself the question why. I believe daydreams have purposes. Human beings seem to appear to be in an emotional cyberspace when they daydream. I believe when someone daydreams, suppressed or repressed feelings are bubbling up in the form of thoughts, and a human being is overcome by those feelings. Their aware, awake outward attention has become preoccupied. Their feelings are taking the place of their cognitive processes. The individual has been overwhelmed by their emotions.

I believe this is also true of the thoughts that the feelings may trigger. It can also work in reverse. Individual's thoughts may have triggered emotion, and the daydreaming is an indication of how the individual is negotiating the thoughts as well.

Daydreaming is also a way a human being takes a "time out" from present time. I think we all just need to take a "time out" from present time so we can rest from, for example, TMI or "too much information."

Hope

We create hope in our lives when we embody and practice those methods that give us productive results. This is authentic hope. When we are hurt, when we cannot handle a situation or circumstance, when we experience overwhelm, we have our methods to expand, evolve, and we then create resiliency in our lives.

When people are in conflict with each other and they make a decision to develop a dialogue based on mutual respect, then hope is created. They learn to create a space where both can express their thoughts and feelings.

Points to Ponder:

When did you last let go of your innermost tensions and just sit down and have a good cry?

What is your awareness, alertness to your feelings, the tensions in your body and how are they associated with your behaviors?

Have you reconnected to your emotional essence?

Have you begun to do your emotional work, to expand, to evolve the beauty of your emotions?

Do you have practical tools/methods in your life that help you help yourself?

What is your emotional quotient? The number 10 being the highest and the number 1 being the lowest.

How empty are you of accumulated tension, and therefore, how full are you of vitality and life energy?

What components of yourself do you need to improve upon?

Are you doing productive inner work for yourself?

What will it take to motivate you do rediscover the beauty of your emotions?

CHAPTER 5

Removing Fear, Maintaining Resiliency, Learning Faith

"We can learn to emotionally surrender our repressed thoughts and feelings of uncertainty in the very moment of that uncertainty!"

"We can learn to embrace a certain thought and establish a certain reality within by taking charge."

"We can establish a thought and feeling of certainty encompassing faith, light, and self-love."

"When we let go and surrender our fears of an unknown and uncertain future, we are then most certain in the acceptance of present time."

"We can embrace a certain heartfelt courage, a sense of emotional and spiritual faith, and a connection with our Divine Creator."

The greatest challenge for humankind is the anxiety of fear emanating from conscious and unconscious mind. Humankind just does not do fear very well! Fears is an acronym for "false evidence appearing real," "false expectations appearing real," and "forget everything and regress." When you are not in charge in the presence of time, fear can sink into one's consciousness and take charge. It can be deadly, debilitating, and impact intelligent thinking and therefore choices! It can raise your blood pressure.

Fear is the most deceptive of emotions. It can creep into any decision making and can reflect feelings bubbling up from the collected repressed unconscious mind. This makes it deceptive because we are unaware of its impact. Fear will almost without doubt create illusion, delusion, and can penetrate our clarity of thought. It is most certainly at the core of most self-defeating behavior patterns. It's the core of most human conflict! Denial is often the result of fear.

When people react to me in an angry manner I immediately think that their anger can be possibly motivated by their fear. I believe that both vanity and self-consciousness is also related to unconscious fear. The feeling of fear is reflective of our inadequacy and insecurity that comes from being hurt. The thought "I'm not good enough" emanates from this fear.

The key is to become alert and aware to and of our thoughts and feelings of fear. We can contradict the feelings by way of our alertness and awareness to our thoughts, feelings, and behaviors.

We contradict fear by way of positive thoughts. We learn to take charge of our cognitive thoughts! We can learn to respond immediately upon a negative thought by invoking a positive one! We must invoke positive thought sufficiently. We must act to do it again and again and again. We can attempt to cope with our fears in this way regardless of our circumstances and situations. Thinking in terms of faith, trust, peace of mind, love, self-love, gratitude, forgiveness, harmony, health, beauty, play can be quite significant in contradicting patterns of fear.

However, it usually is not enough to depend upon our cognitive strength. The key is to enable oneself to effectively contradict the fear. What happens to our tension? We learn to let go of/surrender/release it! We learn to surrender/release it using any method that resonates with ourselves. The ways we can surrender and release our fears could include visualization, rebirthing, meditation, peer counseling, self-talk, taekwondo, etc.

We can listen to cognitive advice from friends, counselors, and psychologists to talk out our fears, to forget them, but it becomes our responsibility to surrender and release them.

Culture of Fear, Culture of Faith

It's important as a teacher to instill a structure of faith in the classroom. It's important as a country to instill a structure of faith in a society. In a structure of faith we can experience transformation, transition, expansion, liberation, knowledge, dynamic flexible intelligence, and thinking. In a structure of fear we experience repression, oppression, depression, suppression, limitation, rigidity, ignorance, and constriction.

There are positive, healthy behaviors to self and to others that need encouragement, and there are unhealthy behaviors that require immediate positive punishment to instill a thought process of change. The teacher in the classroom teaches positive, healthy behaviors. It is a component of their agenda and their employment mission. We do this in the classroom on a continuous basis with children. The result depends upon a variety of variables. The major variable being the degree, depth, and dimension of the distress the kid carries. The key always is to stay alert and aware of one's own behaviors toward the children and primarily to maintain a loving attitude.

Variety of Fears

Fear of Instability and Scarcity

The fear of instability, scarcity, of not having enough may always be a concern. We practice, pray, and use our breath methodologies to master, access, connect, surrender, release, and experience self-forgiveness when we experience fears.

We often use nature as a resource to master this insecurity. We can enjoy a walk along the river or a walk along a beach in the sun, or at sunset. We can pay a visit to the mountains or the desert and experience their beauties. The impact is to relax. We can better connect with feelings and maintain both an alertness and awareness of our feelings with relaxation.

Learning to release fear "well" is pivotal to humankind. Human growth cannot be achieved without learning the lesson of letting go / surrender and the release of fear thoroughly!

Uncertainty

Uncertainty can be a reflection of a hurt or lack of information or knowledge. If the uncertainty is derived because we've been hurt, we can then use our methods/tools to address our feelings. We can then transform our energy into our spiritual faith. We have often been uncertain about making choices, but we have maintained enough faith to take risks in our lives. Spiritual faith is a great provider of courage.

Standing Up for Self

This action usually brings up fear in many of us. Just think of anytime when you needed to speak out, take an action; for example, file a small claim against someone in small claims court. When you acted on your own behalf and fear and terror may have paralyzed you. You may have been overwhelmed with this feeling. It is here where the combination of bioenergetic, primal sound, and circular divine breathing can play a significant role in your liberation from the energy of fear. It is under these circumstances where we can learn to reach out for support from others.

Feelings of Jealousy

Feelings of jealousy can include anger, grief, and sadness. The feelings can come from not getting the attention we needed from the past or in the present. Or not getting the love one has needed.

Often when a new sibling is born the attention is shifted to the new child. The older child who received previously all the attention may now feel impacted. The following thoughts may arise from sibling's feelings of hurt. Why are they rejecting me now? Who is this new person? We hate them! We hate ourselves for being unable to control the situation or circumstances! Why aren't they giving us the attention they have given us before? What have we done wrong? We hate this new person! We want the attention! How dare the new person take our parents love away from us! We're afraid we'll lose our parents' love! The older child needs more attention and love than ever before to deal with new siblings.

This can also happen when our spouse or girlfriend begins to flirt with another man or woman. The significant other may also begin to feel threatened by losing their partner's love and begin to feel unloved, angry, sad, or fearful. They may feel insecure. Men and women have the tendency to become competitive with each other in societies.

We use peer counseling and integrative, divine, circular, cleansing, healing, and transformation breath to access suppressed and repressed feelings of sadness, anger, and fear. We choose to surrender and release them on the exhale and when we surrender and release enough we feel better.

A positive affirmation for jealousy is "We know enough, we have enough, we do enough, and most importantly, we are enough."

Fear and the So-Called Angel of Darkness

Ever since then, all that lies in the past and all that lies in the future pales in comparison to what lies within.

—Lt. Jeffrey L. Quinn
Commenting on his
two fallen comrades
in Mogadishu

It felt terribly eerie that day. It was like the angel of darkness descending upon the city and perhaps the earth. The streets were quieter than usual. Most of the men and women were deployed to the Middle East. They were being deployed to the Iraq war theater. The war was beginning. I sensed the angel of darkness. I could feel its presence. It was in wait. The eeriness felt like it was waiting to take the souls of those who would die in the war. This was of course my thought from the dark sensation that surrounded me. Their death would bring sadness to their loved ones. I felt the sense of that coming emotion! I felt the gloom in the air. It permeated the senses. War is ugly. Death because of war cannot help but to be described as tragic. Those who are distressed and those who are traumatized must reach out for support. Too bottle up feelings within is unhealthy—even those socialized into the process of the military despise the thought of war. I felt sad feeling the impending grief that the war would bring to friends and family of those who will give their lives. I felt the impending psychological trauma the war would bring to its participants. There will be approximately 15 to 20 percent of participating soldiers who will be impacted psychologically by the war! The war will cause emotional wounds suppressed and eventually repressed in one's collected unconscious. War creates the distressful sounds, sights, and smells of gore and destruction. The sensation of evil permeated my senses. The evil was overpowering. There was no denying its presence.

The streets quieter than usual added to the eerie sensation. There were many who were not present. San Diego, California's population consists of many in the military. There was a clear decrease in the number of automobiles on the streets. There were individuals on vacation. Schools were closing for spring break. The estimated Latino population of San Diego County is three hundred thousand of three million residents. Perhaps many of these residents were on their way home or to visit relatives or friends in the country of Mexico. San Diego is a border city. This was perhaps yet another reason.

I had felt the presence of the angel of darkness several times before. Once when I entered my friend's hospital room where he lay diagnosed with Hodgkin's disease, I had sensed eeriness inside his room. My sense was that an untimely dark shadow had come into that space. I sensed that the angel had come for him. The angel's presence was eerie. It was in wait. It was in wait for an impending death. It was facilitating my friend's transition.

Yet again the component of fear is ever present. How does that component reach out and permeate the environment? The component of faith and trust and confidence are impacted by the emotion of fear. There seemed to be an eerie presence in waiting. It was a very eerie feeling. I can only describe the feeling as that of inevitable doom. It felt like a definitive ending. There would be a transition to another state of reality. It was yet another dimension in and of time and space. It was perhaps an opportunity of yet another beginning. I sensed that a soul would be experiencing transition to another dimension. This sense was neither intuition nor instinct. It was just what it was: a sense of present-time reality.

The same feeling existed when in September 2001 the World Trade Center was taken down. The untimely dark shadow had descended to ground zero and to Earth and was in waiting to conduct its untimely, seemingly unnatural natural process of being the catalyst of transition. The days subsequent to the World Trade Center's coming down was filled with the eeriness of what I believe to be the angel of darkness coming to undertake its function in spiritual nature.

Iraq War was about to begin. The strange death feeling was in wait. The angel was coming so that its presence was in preparation to do its work. Its work of the natural guidance and assistance it provides for souls in transition. It's waiting to do its evitable spiritual calling. I sensed that it instinctively knew its purpose. The angel's presence was but a component of a natural process unfolding. It couldn't help but to be present for the inevitable consequences of war.

The angel of darkness is in essence a "good angel" and is just doing its calling on its mission. When we begin to recognize and realize this then we can relinquish our fear of death. We can work with our feelings as a bridge to our spirituality and raise our state of consciousness and arrive at a sense of peace knowing that there is nothing to fear, not even its messenger.

Politics of Fear

We need to determine what fact is, and what is made-up fact that comes from our fears. The United States of America is fighting a war on terror. Politicians can erroneously promote terror by promoting the politics of intimidation and fear. Politicians are human and do make mistakes. They can do this by exploiting terror incidents with the goal of frightening people to think that terror acts will be widespread. The government is responsible to its people and must present a clear history of terror incidents.

The issue of terror in the United States can have ramifications as a political ploy to create the range of feelings and their nuances of insecurity and inadequacy. The reality of the politics of fear can be exaggerated out of proposition for political reasons. Terror is a threat. People need factual information about a clear and present danger of terror. We must all take responsibility and discern the facts about this issue and how the government formulates its policy goals to address this menace.

There have been allegations that policy makers in the administration of the United States Government have placed pressure on the United States Intelligence Community to exaggerate the threat of terror. It has been alleged that the present administration divulged the names of Central Intelligent Agency agents who are unwilling to support erroneous information distributed by top government officials. It has been said that the information communicated has impacted the credibility of Americans employed by the Central Intelligence Agency and created a pattern of mistrust and fear in the war on terror. The government must make its policies clear to contradict any and all fear.

Find the Silence

Find the Silence
Beneath the Sound
And the Stillness from which to move.
In the Silence I find you.
Find the Silence
Beneath the Sound
And the Stillness from which to move
In the Silence I find you.
Here I Am
In the Stillness I find You
Here I Am.

© 2002 by Malaya Rider

Points to Ponder:

What is your alertness/awareness of your individual experience of fear?

Are your behaviors reflective of your unconscious fears?

What issues do you have reflective of your fear?

Are you aware of fears of friends, co-workers, and family?

What awareness do you have of the angel of death?

Do you have an understanding of the politics of fear?

Are you fearful of scarcity, uncertainty, instability, and have feelings of jealousy?

Do you have a high faith quotient?

CHAPTER 6

Transcendence, Transmutation, Transparency, Transformation, and Transition

We are all different. Our biological, genetic, developmental, and environmental experiences are unique to ourselves. Our biological, genetic, developmental experiences reflect our temperament, sensitivities, and personalities. The hurts and traumas that impact one person may impact another person differently. Our worldly experience is unique to ourselves.

We can make the decision for transcendence, transmutation, or transformation of those hurt, traumatized feelings or feelings set in frozen, unfulfilled needs. We can experience these emotions daily, situational or circumstantially. We may not have a choice but to transform ourselves. We must be strong enough to transcend our feelings until we can adjust. Our emotional devastation may be so dramatic that transformation of our distressful feelings through dynamic emotional surrender and release may be necessary.

Transparency and transcendence is created through consistent, focused, effective, and efficient practice of our tools/methods. Transparency and transcendence help us to expand, evolve, heal, liberate ourselves, and to connect to the divine spark within. It helps us to connect with our spiritual power!

We Can Create the Transcendence, Transmutation, Transparency, Transformation, and Transition

We act to gradually develop and use our methods and tools that enable us to experience transparency, transcendence, and transition into healthier constructive behaviors. This removes the walls and obstacles that "get in our way." The emotional transparency becomes visible to us and helps us to surrender and release blockages and feelings more easily. It is like a puzzle that all begins to fall into place. If we choose we can visualize the walls reflective of defense mechanisms and the walls that house our feelings reflective of emotions that do not serve us. The walls begin to disintegrate as we apply our effective tools and methods with focus. Our healing, our consciousness raising, our enlightenment, and the development of our personal power become the light of our infinite breath— our "aloha." We can and do experience bliss much more readily every time we practice a method that resonates with ourselves.

When we obtain a sense of transparency we can better experience the transformation and transcendence of our inner shadows and darkness.

Transparency is created when the walls or defenses slip away and we regain awareness, an awakening, and a rising of consciousness. There is a crossing over. There are emotional barriers to self which begin to dissipate. We begin to visualize and experience ourselves differently. We connect more so with our individuality and spiritual essence. We experience our authenticity. We just feel better, and we have greater awareness in the world.

Our ability to be transparent enables us to connect with any feelings that don't serve us. It enables us to release those feelings naturally. It's fluid. We can then release feelings, and when any negative patterns persist we can then address those patterns much more readily and consistently. The integration, expansion, and evolution of self takes place. The falling away of our defensive walls enables more of the self to grow and materialize.

Often patterns and a myriad of feelings persist. The human being must persist as well. This is a gradual process, a gradual unfoldment. It takes time. It is not surprising that when we begin to experience some success we then begin to experience more joy, love for others, self-love, peace, faith, trust, inner kindness, creativity, harmony, and a wealth of inner abundance. We rediscover pieces and then parts of ourselves that were previously in darkness or shadow.

Transcending It All: We can attempt to transcend both emotional and physical pain through pray and meditation, to some or perhaps to a profound degree. Theater groups and book discussion groups are also excellent ways to transcend one's pain until consciousness rise and transformation take place. We experience new cognitive thoughts and emotional nuances. We have better connections to our senses, creative nature, physical well-being, and more zest for life.

The pain or emotional energy that doesn't serve us tends to return again and again dependent upon the nature, depth, degree (intensity/density), and dimension of the injuries. Ultimately, we may choose to master the ability to feel the range of our emotions and their nuances. We can develop this skill, develop this ability, develop the capacity, develop the emotional muscle to embrace the total and thorough range of all shadow, all darkness that lies within our range of human experience.

It's in learning to be focused, effective, efficient, patient, persistent, and persevering where we can master our emotional component. It's through learning and successfully experiencing methods of transformation and transcendence that will open the door to our emotional bodies that in the final analysis brings us to a point of self-love, realization, and peace. It's here in this or that state of consciousness where we can become true masters of ourselves and our spirituality! It is here where we can arrive and derive divine liberation and freedom. It's there where we make a deepening connection with the divine essence within and without. It's staying connected to our core and our source where we find our spiritual power.

I find practicing a meditation when I have emotions and feelings in my body to transcend works real well for me. I also find it heavenly to practice a meditation subsequent to an emotional release session.

What Is It That We Must Transcend and Transform?

I've encountered a myriad of emotional and psychological patterns that can prevent us from realizing our spiritual power in my peer cocounseling practice. These patterns of behavior arise from conception through adulthood. Often, these patterns are deceiving and can play tricks with our minds. They confuse our ability to think clearly. Instead of feeling our feelings reflective of emotions (anger, fear, and sadness), we may rationalize our pain mentally.

Patterns should not be confused with that which is out of our control. We are born with a set of genetic and biological factors. We then go through a series of psychosocial, psychosexual, and cognitive developments (phases). We must accept that which we cannot change.

The function of patterns is to promote awareness. However, the negative emotional patterns create confusion for us and prevent us from self-realization. We must learn to transcend and transform the following through our cognitive and emotional processing.

Defense mechanisms such as projection, denial, repression, and rationalization that consist of emotional walls resulting from hurts, traumas, and frozen needs are common. They may act to reinforce and protect other emotional/physical hurts and traumas. We may have a pattern of absorbing thoughts and feelings that are negative. The pattern may consist of thinking about stress/distressful experiences, situations, and circumstances.

Patterns may take the form of a prejudice against the opposite gender (male or female). It may be a prejudice of the poor, owning, or working class. Patterns may consist of stereotyping adults, seniors, youth, or children.

Patterns may consist of an attitude of greed, power, jealousy, irrational guilt, denial, and self-denial. We may be ignoring or denying our addictions and problems.

Our pattern of beliefs is the result of our socialization process. It could come from irrational, unfulfilled needs. Patterns can affect our views of race, culture, and nationality. We can be impacted by other human beings who are well meaning but are misguided by their advice to us. There are others' points of view and experience that may be shared in a well-meaning way but have a negative impact upon us. Suggestions, opinions, and meaningless questions can get in the way of our spiritual power. It may emanate from ignorance, insecurity, peer pressure, or economic depression.

Our body language can display our defense mechanisms and our defensive attitudes. Our body language can reflect our resistance to feeling our emotions. Our intellectual resistance is yet another pattern that prevents us from feeling our emotions. We are beings who are too often in our heads and not in touch with the emotional aspect of our bodies and spirits.

We create patterns of gossip and have our individual agendas. We have projections of thoughts, opinions, beliefs, belief systems, and judgments (both internal and external judgments of self). There are attitudes of self-loathing, codependences, socialization, and the indoctrination of individuals by institutions.

Ego (an acronym for "edging God out") and fear get in the way of self-acceptance. They are also involved in the avoidance of admitting that we have made a mistake. There is another "ego" (acronym for "embracing Godly omniscience"). We embrace a godlike *awareness* in the world.

All of the above can create illusions and we can delude ourselves when we are impacted by destructive patterns. These patterns can prevent our transcendence and transformation. Patterns addressed with focused, effective, efficient, and disciplined methods and tools can foster our reemergence and rebirth. However, there remains a significant human quality that is necessary for our transcendence and transformation. What works are people being there for one another in an empathetic and compassionate way. We are then able to begin the process of self-realization and self-love. We do need support from others to facilitate transformation from negative patterns and beliefs.

We Come to know Our Vulnerabilities, Inadequacies, and Insecurities

We can have a goal to learn and know our vulnerabilities, inadequacies, and insecurities through our experiences. We can choose our experiences to come to a greater understanding of those attributes. We can develop the tools and the methods to come to negotiate those attributes consistently, effectively, and with focus. Again, it may be possible to choose. We can choose to use these steps assertively to address our vulnerabilities, inadequacies, and insecurities. We can know them by staying alert and aware of our ten bodies in our pyramid and how they are impacted by our actions and our behaviors. Are our actions, behaviors, situations, circumstances nurturing and healthy to our natures? Are our actions, behaviors, situations, and circumstances impacted in an unhealthy way as it reflects our unique natures?

Maintaining Balance and Focus

How do we stay focused? We stay focused through our commitment to our self-realization and therefore liberation. We experience a gradual process to enable us to expand, evolve, and encourage and add to our spiritual power and growth.

Denial and Self-Denial

Awareness is the greatest antidote to denial. When one finds one self in conflict with another individual or with oneself, awareness may begin the path to resolution of the issue. Self-exploration may be essential.

Awareness is not always necessary when one clearly and intuitively knows what is correct. That is the gut feelings and clear thought processes. The clear thought process comes when naturally the thought connects concretely with the feeling. "I am clearly in the knowing."

The religious institution invited me to speak about my first book *I Dare to Heal with Compassionate Love*. The book presentation had been scheduled and cancelled several times, and I had no great expectations of the presentation occurring. However, I was wrong. The clergy mailed a flyer to its congregation saying what I would be speaking about. They promoted the event as the "ultimate challenge." I had misgivings about speaking to a group from their congregation since I knew that their beliefs weren't of the "mind, body, spirit, soul" connection. Nevertheless, I was encouraged to speak before the group of approximately twenty people. I had invited several friends to my book presentation.

A Case of Ultimate Challenge

The facilitator, a clergy member, stated that Mr. Vorensky was to have twenty minutes and then those present would have an opportunity to ask questions. I explained to the group about transpersonal methods (meaning personal growth methods relating to learning about self beyond the superficial mask or appearance) and how some of these methods were congruent with their beliefs. I explained how may of the healing and personal growth methods were effective in addressing our inner frontiers. However, I could sense enormous denial taking place among those present. I used an example of methods that can be used to surrender and release the feeling of grief by speaking about my guardian father who had passed away just two days before. I had stayed with my guardian father until I had witnessed his last breath. After his death, I had emptied myself of grief and felt that the time had come to celebrate life. When I stated as such a woman in the group reacted and said, "How could you go out and enjoy yourself when someone had passed away?" I explained patiently to her that I had used a method that enabled me to surrender and release enormous amounts of grief and that it was time to celebrate life. She then grabbed her heart and claimed to be having a panic attack. My book presentation abruptly ended when the other women present took control, and I was rudely unable to continue. My friend who I invited to the book presentation reacted strongly and spoke up in my defense. It was to no avail because my friend was ignored. When I protested to the clergy that the women in the audience reacted and that other women took control, the clergy took their side, and I was asked not to return to the religious institution again. I invited the clergy to raise its consciousness and learn about the mind, body, spirit, soul connection. Several weeks passed and the clergy realized the benefits of my presentation and E-mailed their encouragement.

I can only reflect upon this experience as a group of individuals who were in denial since I had given the same presentation approximately forty times in person and on radio. This presentation was focused on methods that were reflective of their holy inscribed pages. I responded by E-mail to the clergy saying that some of the congregation reacted to the "ultimate challenge" by being in "ultimate denial."

Addictions

Healing from Morphine Addiction

I had complications upon receiving a total knee joint replacement. I was treated with morphine and extra strength vicodin. I became addicted to both these drugs. I cured my addiction to morphine and vicodin through emotional release methods. I experienced the intense hot and cold sweats, the chattering, and the shaking. I would not let up when the strong feelings came. I persisted until the feelings of morphine and vicodin addiction dissipated.

Points to Ponder:

Are you aware of or alert to the emotional walls and inhibitions that have come to create personality rigidities in your relationships and your life?

Are the personal growth methods/tools that you use adequate to create a transparency and transcendence of your emotional issues?

Are you willing to do what it takes to invoke the necessary methods/tools to go for transformation?

Are you fully aware of those components in your consciousness that hinder you from self-realization and realizing your divinity within?

Do you experience an authenticity of awareness?

Have you ever made a presentation to a group of people where you sensed a profound sense of denial?

Can you vision your own distressful experiences and envision those issues that require direct attention through transformation.

Can you vision issues in your life reflective of your individual dips, bumps, potholes, and craters that require transcendence?

CHAPTER 7

The Dynamics of Healing Sound

Primal and Primordial Sound

The power of corroboration breaks down the walls.
—George Tenet
Former Director
Central Intelligence Agency

We learn the difference and the use of both primal and primordial sound to succeed on our journey into the steps of taking spiritual power and experiencing enlightenment. The sounds are significant because methods such as peer counseling and other counseling methods, conscious healing breath work, devotional singing and chanting play a significant role in our gradual self-realization, cognitive and emotional growth.

There is a difference in the depth, degree (intensity and density of emotion), and the emotional dimension of experiencing primordial, emotional sound and primal sound. The connection with these sounds is a precursor to emotional surrender and release by way of the circular breath. We definitively *know* the difference between these two sounds through our experience with consistent, persistent, and patient practice through our gradual understanding of the range of our issues stored within.

The emotional vibration of frequency is most definitively emotionally deeper and clearly different at the primordial frequency. It is this sound that is so powerful in accessing, surrendering, and releasing feelings associated with emotional and physical traumas.

Primal and primordial sounds are essential tools used when making daily dramatic emotional adjustments and growth to a variety of different situations and circumstances. There are periods of time when I'm employed as a substitute teacher. I teach kindergarten through the fourth grade in English and Spanish, nonsevere and emotionally challenged classes, special day classes, adult GED, and English as a Second Language classes. I must make psychological adjustments in my teaching methods when I'm employed at four or five different classes each week because of the variety of groups. The primal and primordial use of sound helps me to surrender and release the stress associated with making emotional adjustments.

Crystal Bowl Vibrations

We use crystal bowl vibrations as a door opener and as a catalyst to attain transparency, transcendence, transformation, and transition.

Elivia Melody's passion is helping others to heal through her expertise as a musician playing crystal bowl vibrations. The variety of frequency of the crystal bowl vibrations' healing is expedited through her background and experience as a healer.

The crystal bowl vibrations expedite attunements to and for the individual's specific needs for healing. She has the background and experience over many years in achieving this purpose. The immediate effect of personal sound attunements is for the individual to experience stress release and relaxation.

Elivia Melody is an outgoing, vibrant spirit. I have known her for several years. I heard her as a musician for the first time four years ago when with my eyes closed became absorbed by the sound and frequencies reflective of her expertise through the healing catalyst of the crystal bowl vibrations.

She stated, "I have a strong belief that there is a need for healing to take place both in an effortful and in an effortless, joyful, and successful way. Our beings are absorbed into the variety of frequencies by listening to the sounds of the crystal bowl vibrations. Meditating and absorbing their sounds can only aid in the healing of an individual."

When I listen to the playing of the crystal bowls, they trigger both suppressed, repressed feelings and tensions within me. The sounds that emanate from the playing of the crystal bowls also function as a catalyst to assist me to adjust suppressed, repressed feelings and tensions that are triggered.

Elivia explains crystal bowl sound healing in the following paragraph: Crystal bowl sound healing called attunements are so effective for several reasons. Their tones have the ability to give you this total tune-up! On the minutest level, our physical body is crystalline in structure, so the proper resonance of specific crystal bowl tones can move our bodies very quickly into balance. Crystal bowl tones are calibrated to resonate at exact frequencies for specific energy center—chakras—governing our energy body. When the tones are sounded, our own energy centers will begin to match the vibratory rate of the tones of the crystal bowls. They will then send this adjustment out to the rest of the mental, emotional, physical, and spiritual energy bodies. Our body begins literally to match the rhythm of the frequency of the crystal bowl's tone. Just as you might tap your toe as you happily listen to music with a strong rhythm, the energy body happily follows along with the crystalline rhythm of the singing bowls. This process is called entrainment.

Gayatri Mantra

The Gayatri Mantra is a Sanskrit mantra that has very powerful healing sounds. Deval Premal chants the Gayatri Mantra in her CD *The Essence*. The mantra has helped a myriad of people to access suppressed and repressed feelings by way of just listening and receiving the healing, relaxing sounds. When the mantra is used with circular connected healing breath, vini yoga (yoga of the breath) or other circular breathing methods, the impact cannot help but to be a loving experience.

Jazz, Blues, Baroque, and Opera

Using a variety of music is another way of moving shadow and dark energy out of the body.

The music of jazz and blues touch us in its "feeling" form and in its feeling structure of emotional frequencies. The sounds move shadow and dark emotion out of our body. When we listen to the sound of the harp we become connected to and begin to resonate with the angelic nature of our beings.

I love the passion and the vibrancy expressed in the musical film *Chicago.* The musical steams with life itself and is a magnificent reflection of the creative essence.

Baroque music can often be heard to calm infant children. It's wonderful to listen to the power of a soprano or baritone at the opera. They just emanate both primal and primordial sound. We cannot help but to acknowledge the reflection of wholeness that is represented in the sounds of their primal, primordial essence. It is the power of their sounds reflective of their vibrations coming to us as gifts from their centers of wholeness and their innate powerful essence.

Points to Ponder:

What sounds resonate with you?
Can those sounds aid you in any healing or personal growth, want, need or desire that you may consider?
Would you ever consider attending a concert where musicians perform with crystal bowl vibrations?

Have you ever listened to the primal sounds of opera singers?

How have you been impacted by the singers at the opera in an emotionally healing way?

Are you impacted by the sounds of the nature?

What sounds cause you dissonance?

CHAPTER 8

Nature versus Nurture, Imprinting (Chronic Distress) and Frozen Needs

The debate in psychology often occurs whether human beings' behaviors are either the result of nature or is of the nurturing we receive. We are clearly the result of our genetic, biological, developmental, and environmental makeup. I believe we are the result of both nature and nurture. I believe this to be so based upon my thirty-eight years of personal experience practicing a variety of healing and developmental methods.

I believe "imprinting" of a distress pattern (chronic distress) can take place anytime, but in particular, imprinting of a pattern can take place in the formative years. The imprinting is usually caused by a traumatizing experience that is imprinted on our nature. The result is, throughout our lives when similar circumstances and situations present themselves, those circumstances and situations cause the triggering of emotion and the feelings around that initial imprinting trauma. The range of dark feelings attempts to take charge of the human being. Tensions are created within the nervous system. It can feel like immediate darkness and sheer hell. The emotional body is overwhelmed and a part of it shuts down. A part of ourselves is in permanent shutdown, and we experience emotional separation. We are emotionally disconnected. This only occurs if we are not aware, alert, and awake of the triggering of our imprinted patterns. We can address the issue immediately when we are alert and aware. The triggering of the imprinting trauma creates a situation for the human being where he/she can use healing methods and tools. Methods need to be used with focus, effectively, and efficiently to emotionally surrender the triggered feelings reflective of particular circumstances and situations. The result is personal growth, flexibility of thought, adjustment, and adaptation in the present. There is a dynamic growth in human intelligence because of our rational response to the restimulated feelings. When we use emotional surrender and release methods and tools we then have an opportunity to connect with our spirituality. This is because emotion is one bridge to the connection with a divine entity. Praying is yet another method we can use to connect with a divine entity when shadow and dark feelings are restimulated. Imprinting leads us to a discussion of frozen needs and how they can emanate from imprinting as well.

Samuel

The kindergarten teacher approached me regarding Samuel. He was Caucasian with brown hair and brown eyes and was anxious with his verbal and bodily reactions upon human contact. The teacher claimed he was diagnosed as being attention deficit. I explained to the teacher that one of the causes of attention deficit was "frozen needs."

I worked with Samuel as a teacher. My immediate impression was in fact Samuel's being attention deficit was the result of just such "needs." I intuitively understood his distress because of my experience with suppressed and repressed feelings.

Samuel couldn't focus his attention long enough on any one task without an overpowering emotional need to move on to the next object. He just couldn't sit still and focus his attention on any one task. He required a great deal of attention from me and others to help him complete a goal at a time.

Those Unfulfilled Frozen Needs

Filling one's own needs: We all have primary needs. Primary needs are emotional in nature. These include sleep, food, nurturing in the form of touch, human empathy and warmth, sensitivity, understanding, being listened to, receiving attention, the sense of our caretaker's presence, being held and embraced, and social contact in community. We have a need for caring attention, to be listened to. We have a need for warmth nurturing in others' behavior to us. We have a need for kindness and understanding. We have a need for emotional and intellectual development. We have a need for eye contact with our caregiver, warmth, the sound, the tone of voice of secure verbal contact, for closeness. We get hungry and have a need to be feed. We can learn nurturing through our experience of being feed. We have a need for sleep. We need to learn limits to our behaviors or a secure structure where we can experience a sense of security. These are many of our primary needs in our formative years from conception through the age of six. What are frozen needs? They are all unfulfilled and disordered emotional needs. They are manifested in our feelings of, to some extent, separation, abandonment, and betrayal. Our frozen chronic needs create a sense of separation, abandonment, and betrayal of ourselves. We become disconnected from ourselves because of them! The feelings reflective of the emotions create a disconnection from and of the self!

What are secondary needs? We need food, housing, physical space (own bedroom for example), clothing, and enough income for other necessities. We also have material needs (autos, money, health care).

Frozen needs are also those needs left unfulfilled in our formative years. When needs are not met, the needs translate into tensions and energy that does not serve us. It becomes both suppressed and repressed pain. My experience is that deep-seated emotional tensions emanate from repressed feelings. The hurts can be traumatizing. Our earliest unfulfilled needs in our formative years of our dips, bumps, potholes, and craters translate into tensions in our teen, adolescent, and adult years. Tensions can keep coming from within moment to moment. They build within and shout out to be addressed by us.

When these needs are consistently unmet we experience pain. We don't understand how the pain accumulates and is suppressed until it's repressed. The repressed pain accumulates and creates "frozen needs." These frozen needs manifest themselves into anxiety, depression, self-defeating behaviors, destructive behaviors, and possibly additive behaviors later in our lives.

The pain reflective of frozen needs can contain the range of feelings of sadness through grief, anger through rage, and fear through terror, and a myriad of nuances, depths, degrees (intensity and density of feelings within the body), and dimensions. They show or reveal themselves as tensions. There is the emotional pain of profound "need" that exits.

I have found that the solution to "frozen needs" is to embrace them initially in a gradual use of processes and ultimately perhaps through the use of both primordial (original sound) and primal sound. The sounds permeate the frozen needs and the feelings well up from within. We learn to surrender and release the feelings through a variety of methods including exhaling by way of the integrated, circular, connected, divine, healing, transformational breath.

The result is when enough work is completed we potentially "liberate" ourselves from our tensions and those energies that do not serve us. We experience more harmony, happiness, and peace.

Samuel's unmet needs—his frozen needs—have manifested themselves into those needs being "acted out" in the form of self-defeating and unruly attention deficit behavior. The behavior involves anxiousness in responding to questions. He has inattention and has conflicts with other children.

Frozen needs are locked away in repressed feelings reflective of emotion in our collected unconscious. We can become alert and aware of them by developing our intuition—our third eye chakra.

We learn to use our methods/tools to address our emotional tensions within so that we learn to transform our issues to free more of ourselves from our shadow, darkness, and black emotional holes where an abundance of feelings can be found.

We go for integration of ourselves. We connect divinely with those parts of ourselves as we are successful in surrendering and releasing feelings reflective of those specific emotions. We experience a freeing up a part of ourselves that was formerly shut down. We then experience a sense of redemption! We then experience a sense of stillness, peace, happiness, and more harmony within.

My employment as a teacher brought the reality of children's frozen needs for attention through their "acting out" which is reflective of their "behaviors" in the classroom. It was their manifestations that caused my profound understanding of the emotional devastation within children. Emotional devastation is usually incomprehensible to those who have not surrendered and released feelings reflective of tensions and have not remembered of having a good cry.

A lot of the acting out comes from children's experience of separation, abandonment, and betrayal. The bonding between the infant and the adults were inadequate, unstable, and fragmented. The emotional tragedy is ever present and reflective of childhood depression. The needs are exhibited in many ways, shapes, and forms in the classroom. It is so sad to see it exhibited. The solution is to find ways where children can begin to address the pain in their lives. *Love* is certainly helpful but reinstilling personal power for children requires the child like the adult to address his pain energy. Children can begin to learn simple circular breath techniques in kindergarten. I've seen teachers instruct small children in circular breathing. Children can gradually learn to connect with and learn to surrender their pain energy naturally. Children like adults must have some prerequisite attention to achieve this optimal goal. They need enough attention to connect with their feelings in a way that best resonates with themselves. It's not good enough to say that children will grow out of it! The hurt and traumas are locked into the personality.

Embracing Our Tensions and Feelings Reflective of Our Frozen Needs

When we embrace in a nurturing way our unmet past or present emotional needs, we experience a letting-go, release, and liberation of those feelings that have been triggered. Embracing ourselves and being in service to and embracing others are significant steps in our enlightened path and reacquiring our spiritual power toward our goal of wholeness.

The action of embracing those spaces within ourselves filled with shadow and darkness can only aid us in our liberation and freedom. When others embrace us, grant us empathy and compassion through our connection with them we also experience our willingness to let go, and dare to experience a release and perhaps a step toward our liberation. We act in the same way to others and help them to liberate themselves as well! It is our decision in the final analysis that makes the human difference.

What is it to embrace? I believe it is to bring compassionate attention, alertness, awareness to all types of feelings associated with the frozen needs. We learn to love the hurt feelings associated with the distress. We learn to love the feelings by creating the emotional space so they are primed and ready for surrender and release. We learn to love ourselves, invoking new innovative tools and methods that resonate with ourselves. We embrace those tools/methods that permit and allow emotion to flow. There is no holding in, holding on, holding tight, and holding tough. We develop a posture of surrender and an attitude of letting go.

Types of Feelings: Stuck Feelings—Reflective Frozen Needs

Stuck feelings are a sure sign of a frozen need. It's the toughest feeling for an individual to embrace. We need a lot of loving to address effectively, efficiently, and with focus. It's cognitively very deceptive. The patterns play mind tricks and are deceiving. Many of us hold on to stuck feelings because of codependences, a sense of not being good enough and internal and external judgments.

We are responsible for filling our primary and secondary needs in our adult life. We are also responsible for paying attention to addressing the frozen needs that exist in our emotional body. These are the feelings for closeness, warmth, touch, security, and attention that we know perhaps intuitively and perhaps feel emotionally those needs that are left unmet.

We usually dare not place attention on these needs because it is too, too painful to . . . well, go there! We unconsciously attempt to get these needs met through others. We may unconsciously say to ourselves that others (in particular our significant other) must fill this need that is why we are in a relationship with them. They must make us happy! As soon as we put these frozen needs or any needs into the relationship with other people, especially our significant other, then these frozen needs reflect directly back on ourselves and can cause conflict in our relationships and within ourselves. We must maintain a realization that our partners have the right to say no. We can be compassionately supportive of our partners and help them help themselves to surrender and let go and emote their feelings. Hearing the word "no" from your partner may not be a "feel good" situation!

We must take responsibility for helping ourselves. If and when our feelings are reflective of frozen needs, if and when our feelings are triggered and are restimulated, then we can choose and decide to feel pain energies. The realization is that others are not here to make us happy. It is our responsibility to nourish ourselves and make our own selves happy!

The Embracing Conscious Hug

When we embrace our dips, bumps, potholes, craters, and frozen needs, it helps us to learn surrender and eventually release. When we learn to embrace pain in any component of our self, we help to free up that part of ourselves and prepare our body to experience the surrender and release of those energies that do not serve us. We embrace a physical hurt with tender loving care and give it attention. This aids in our healing of that injury. The key is to give the injury enough attention. When we embrace our soul in a tender loving way, give it enough attention, and nurture it we free up our soul from that pain. There is divine healing that takes place. There is a raised consciousness, there is empowerment, and there is an increase in our personal and spiritual power which alters our enlightened state.

The frozen chronic need, though difficult to resolve with committed work, can be resolved! I've worked to resolve this issue consistently and have met with much success. The key to its resolution is that we resolve not to "give up" but to keep on releasing the emotion of the suppressed and repressed feelings.

The best indication of the frozen need is if and when the feelings are triggered. The energy is felt and we address immediately the energy by using our methods and tools that we have developed over time. I've been successful in addressing feelings of frozen need because of my repeated surrender and release of needy, profound feelings.

The nature of chronic need has a variety of components. Once again frozen needs are formed usually in our formative years from prebirth to age five or six. The feelings that can trigger frozen needs in present time are fear, anger, or sadness. I believe the most common trigger is fear. This can trigger the energy of pain reflective of the need!

The issue could be scarcity. The insecurity could be environmental, developmental—unemployment, underemployment—or inadequate economic wealth. These reasons can trigger the energy of pain from the past.

When one hasn't received proper nurturing as a youth, as one grows older, that need, for example, of touch has become frozen in that period of time when the need was present. The need takes the form of being triggered in present time and one feels the pain of that need.

I've learned to negotiate the suppressed and repressed feelings associated with frozen need! I use the rhythmic, connected, circular, spiritual breath to go into the repressed feelings of frozen need! The circular breath will always in all ways take me into, permit me, allow me to go through and release the suppressed, profound feelings associated with a need for security!

We are forever telling our stories around our frozen needs. We learn that in telling our stories we become stuck and generate yet more emotional energy within the details. We seldom find a solution to our frozen needs by telling our story. The solution is found by experiencing the feelings reflective of the emotions within and around the needs.

Impulse behavior can become compulsive along with an aggressive personality trait. It can then become hurtful to others. The impulse behavior can emanate from its own hurtful experiences. Compulsive behavior can emanate from frozen chronic need as well.

Overwhelm, Shutdown, Withdrawal, and Acting Out

There are times when we are overwhelmed with stress or distress feelings triggered by chronic need or other traumas and we emotionally shut down, withdraw or act out our needs. Kids act out their needs quite often in the classroom. It's during these times when we can learn to take charge, take the time, and use our methods/tools to remove our restimulated feelings out of our body and expand ourselves. We can choose to respond rationally and invoke methods/tools that work for us and choose not to withdraw or act out.

Points to Ponder:

What imprinted chronic distress patterns are you aware of?

Are you aware of your tensions within emanating from frozen chronic, unfulfilled, repressed feelings?

Are you emotionally frustrated and stuck and cannot see your way clear out of frozen chronic need?

Are you willing to begin addressing your frozen chronic needs?

Do you have enough methods/tools or processes that will begin to address them?

CHAPTER 9

Nuances of Our Spirit

We have a joyful, expressive, energized, zestful, creative, intuitive, dynamic, positive, emotional, empowered, and above all completely lovable spirit. Our spirit is empowered by our breath! If and when our energy is freed up from frozen needs—suppressed and repressed feelings—then our energy is free to flow fully, and we can express ourselves through our life-given energy of the breath! We are infused with the breath of spirit when we are born, and we are poised from birth to radiate that enthusiasm from the beginning of our lives. We expect to be in charge of our world. What happens is we get hurt. We are impacted by hurts in many subtle and unaware ways by others and in society. We may or may not be cognitively conscience of being hurt, but emotionally we are impacted by painful feelings in our body. The feelings take up emotional space within. We may, for example, have experienced our breast feeding in a controlled, sad, or painful way. This may have caused us to develop anxiety or a need to control as we mature. There may or may not be a myriad of personality manifestations of our hurt. Our lives are not necessarily so smooth. All doesn't unfold smoothly because we are impacted by our genetic, biological, environmental, and developmental experience within our inner world in the wide world. The hurt gets in the way and impacts our free-flowing, natural, inborn energy. The hurt impacts our nature.

La Chispa Divina (The Divine Spark)

We connect with our inner radiance when we are proactive. When we endow our spirit with prayers, for example, we can develop spiritually.

It is a life-transforming experience to connect with one's divine spark. Our everyday suffering from physical or emotional pain becomes bearable if and when we determine their solutions. This is especially true of pain emanating from physical challenges. We can then use our tools and methods to free ourselves once again— deepen and strengthen our connection with the light. It is here where we receive the empowerment of infinite life itself. Our divine source never extinguishes even though death itself may occur. This realization is apparent when we have discovered its energy within. When we stay connected to its light it helps us to maintain our life's purpose and therefore helps us to maintain our focus.

As we develop greater depth, degree, and dimension in our connection with *la chispa divina* we understand that the voice of the divine speaks to us through our infinite soul that contains an infinite light and love. The greater emotional clarity we achieve, the greater we free our soul, deepen our connection with the divine entity, and the clearer, more profound, the more frequent, and the more lovingly we experience the divine voice.

The clearing of negative emotion, stress, physical pain energy, and any emotional energy that does not serve our well-being is the most significant act we can take in purifying our souls. It allows for the divine voice to speak in a loving way to and through us.

The clearing of the emotion around our heart brings about physical health and an open heart so we can extend empathy and compassion to ourselves and know courage and connection with, to, and for ourselves. This is the essence of love itself.

Community Divine Spark

We can achieve a profound connection in the community to a community divine spark through a group-healing, life-giving, and transformational divine breath experience.

Divine Celebration of the Circular Dance with the Men in Black

There is a celebration of welcoming in the queen of the Sabbath and the divine spirit by the sacred teaching of the Jewish people—the Torah. I have participated in a Orthodox Chabad Friday Sabbath Service at sundown. I enjoy singing prayers in the Hebrew and Aramaic language. After a beautiful prayer, the Orthodox rabbi celebrates the beginning of the Sabbath by leading the congregation as he claps and as we walk behind him while we create a warm, loving, celebrative circle. The circle celebrates the divine spirit and the beginning of its day of rest, the seventh day. This symbolic ritual is open to all!

The Rededication

There is a metaphysical meaning to the Hebrew holiday of Chanukah. The word itself in the English language means rededication. The holiday is a rededication of the temple in Jerusalem. It is a rededication of one's faith as well. The Macabees were a group of Jewish fighters who rose up and liberated the Jewish nation from Greek oppressors. The Greek oppressors desecrated the temple of the Jewish people by bringing pigs into the sanctuary. The Macabees liberated the Jewish people by fighting against overwhelming odds.

The temple was liberated from the Greeks, and the liberators found but one cask of pure oil intact. The cask was said to hold enough oil but for one day. It was written that a miracle (seeing of the light) occurred and the oil lasted eight days. The temple was rededicated to the Jewish people and its god.

The holiday takes place in the month of December around the twenty-first, the shortest day in daylight hours. The menorah represents bringing light into the wide world at the darkest period of the year. I can only speculate that it also represents bringing light into those parts of the self where emotional hurt and trauma have harbored shadow and darkness. We have our own rededication (rebirth)—bringing light to where shadow and darkness previously occupied that emotional space. We also rededicate and expand the divine light within and reconnect with the divine light without.

The number 7 and the number 9 have spiritual significance. There are nine candles that form the menorah which I speculate has a transpersonal significance. "Transpersonal" is a metaphysical word meaning "beyond," "beyond the mask." We can go beyond the surface to experience both the suppressed and repressed emotion. We go beyond the mask to dissolve feelings emanating from frozen needs and traumatizing feelings of genetic, biological, and developmental imprinting (chronic distress) of the self. We can go through and into the suppressed and repressed emotion to connect with the feelings that take space in our emotional body in order to surrender and release the shadows and darkness reflective of that emotion. We then are able to shed a renewed "spiritual light" into the wide world.

Tradition says that the number 7 is very significant. This is also true of seven of the nine candles on the menorah. Here are some examples of the significance of the number 7 as it relates to the body, mind, soul, spiritual concept. There are seven days in the week; God took six days to create the world and on the seventh day God rested; seven years for King Solomon to complete his temple; seven significant chakras; the seven faculties of time, dark, light, image, focus, I-Am, and motive, the seven minds of body, feeling, desire, rightness, reason, I-ness, and selfness; seven deadly sins; seven sisters (constellation of the Pleiades), and seven gods of luck in Japanese folk tradition; the Jewish practice of seven days of sitting in honor of the passing away of a beloved mother or father.

The eighth candle is the candle beyond the seventh in the menorah. I'd like to speculate that it is symbolic of a human being going into and through those repressed and suppressed feelings of shadow and darkness and through the manifestations of release and thereby experiencing an evolution, expansion, and possibly a revolution— a greater integration of the components of self. We achieve a greater sense of well-being.

The ninth candle is the gate keeper. It is because we have experienced and brought light into the shadows, darkness, and black holes of self by manifesting the surrender/release of feelings and thereby creating the spiritual bridge for us to experience divinity within and without. We open the door to the ninth gate and we enter into divine light! We expand and evolve the crown chakra.

The Padmacahay Foundation Reiki Tummo Meditation

This process is an integration of Reiki and so-called Tummo or a rising of energy without the breath and accesses the stored energy or Kundalini (awakening) in the spine in order to cleanse the shadow and dark feelings. It is a form of divine practice that focuses on the preparation of the physical, mental, and emotional inner self for cleansing.

The meaning of "Rei" is translated as "God's wisdom" and "Ki" is translated as "universal life force energy." The hand of the practitioner transfers the universal life force energy to the individual who receives the "healing life force energy." Reiki works on the spiritual, physical, mental, and soul levels of the human being. Reiki has many benefits. It relieves pain, promotes creativity, strengthens the immune system, enhances personal awareness, strengthens intuition, and enhances meditation. The focus in Reiki in the practice of Reiki Tummo is to focus and awaken in a safe way the so-called Tummo, Kundalini or stored energy and to cleanse that stored energy in our chakras (coiled energies). The chief chakra lives in our spines. Reiki Tummo also uses at one level of practice the profound power of meditation.

The Kundalini Reiki practitioner performs so-called attunements to remove energy blockages in the body that can be caused by physical, emotional, or spiritual ills. There are three main attunements. The first attunement opens the healing channels to allow channeling of Reiki energy. The hand, crown, and heart chakras are opened and strengthened. One is trained to heal from a distance and to perform a complete healing.

In Kundalini Reiki level two, the main energy channel is opened in a gentle way, illuminating the so-called Kundalini "fire" at the root chakra, and the energy of awakening reaches the chakra in the solar plexus. It is at level two where one learns a specific meditation. This increases the strength of the flame in the Kundalini energy. The result is a cleansing in all the coils of energies or chakras.

The third level of Kundalini Reiki known as the master level strengthens the throat, solar plexus, hara, and root chakras. They are all opened and the Kundalini fire reaches up and out of the crown chakra. There is a so-called full rising of the Kundalini energy that takes place. One is taught at this stage to attune crystals and other objects, so they act as Reiki channels.

The benefits of Kundalini Reiki include balancing all energy systems in the human body, strengthening the flow of energy in the body, cleansing of traumas, regenerating human DNA, cleansing birth trauma caused by the birth process, harmonizing the so-called karmic band between a human being and a specific location, and removing blockages from past life experiences.

One is taught to pass on the three levels of Kundalini Reiki, and one learns to increase the strength of all the attunements with consistent, persistent practice and surrendering and releasing energy in the body that doesn't serve one's well-being.

Through continued and repeated practice, one becomes successful in learning intuitively the nuances of surrender/release of both emotion and the ability to go into / go through / surrender and release energy that does not serve one's well-being. It brings about a connection with and deepens a connection with the divine spark.

Elevation of Spirit

The path is to address, connect, access, go into, release, surrender, and experience bliss and joy! I do this with focus, effectively and efficiently! I go into the range of emotions. They include the sadness through the grief, the anger through the rage, and the fear through the terror!

The sensation of using the breath and experiencing the depth and degrees of emotion is totally fascinating. I can feel the emotional depths and degrees by the slow and gradual release after the pulling in of the breath. I can feel the hurts, the emotional traumas, and most importantly, clearly sense the imprinting (chronic distress) vividly! I can connect with the ranges of feelings as I described previously. It's a remarkable experience!

Please remember our discussion of the concept of emotional dimension. The dimension of the hurt and or trauma takes the form of limiting our emotional time and space! We have less slack when we get hurt! The more release we experience, the greater sense of added emotional time and space we experience! There is more emotional space to experience more of ourselves "living in the present."

We have more slack, more attention for others and the world around us!

Our hurts, traumas, our bumps, dips, potholes, and craters have dimensional form! We can experience this form in relationship to the depth and degree of the emotional ranges! We can experience this form in relationship to the nuances of those ranges!

We can experience irritation, frustration, anger, and finally, rage in its depths, degrees, and other dimensions. The sounds can be different. The release of the emotions can be different. We can use the divine primal and primordial sound to penetrate feelings of deep hurt or trauma. We can experience a broken heart, and we can feel the anger of betrayal. We can feel its sadness and experience the abandonment. We feel fear, and we can begin to tremble or experience the anxiety of separation.

The primal and primordial sounds in and for themselves are not emotional releases. The divine sounds help to penetrate the hurt and or trauma. It's like lightning and thunder. The lighting and thunder come before the rain, the hot and/or cold sweats, and other physiological manifestations.

The stomach becomes a pump. The pelvic chakra is where a great deal of emotion is harbored. It is in this chakra where the most powerful of emotions emanate. The emotions come like waves upon the shore. The connected circular healing breath is performed again and again when we begin the pulling in of breath and then a going into, going through, surrender, and release. This circular breathing is performed again and again with each release! The more we trust the process, the more we relax and the better the circular connected healing breath works. It's exciting and euphoric to experience the emotions released in a relaxed body state. Our spirit becomes naturally connected with the universal spirit! It's truly a wonder! We connect with our spiritual power!

The repair of our physical body begins, and we begin to feel better. We elevate our spirit. The elevation of spirit happens naturally with each release of emotion. We experience joy, love, and bliss!

There are times when we experience ego (edging God out) beliefs, thoughts, distractions, judgments, and defense mechanisms. This is resistance we must put aside or penetrate. We use the oxygenating bioenergetic breath to accomplish this. We perform several exercises with power breathing to begin to create the emotional space for us to go into, go through, surrender, and release emotion! We enjoy playing spiritual music to help us along with the oxygenating of the body and the bioenergetic exercises. We usually do bioenergetic exercises to begin oxygenating the body.

We elevate our spirit during this process. We open our heart chakra by way of the circular breath! It is in the heart chakra where we experience the freeing up of our ability to feel compassion and love! These are essential qualities in order to elevate our spirit! In elevating our spirit we connect with the Universal Godly Spirit. Spiritually, we have embraced a higher power.

This is a process that unlocks the door to the soul! We can view it with colorful infinite freedom. We can have an out-of-body experience! The soul becomes purified. We feel loved. It's a miraculous experience!

An ultimate goal is a conscious state where one integrates within the self an "authentic peace of mind." This is regardless of one's practical situation, i.e., money, employment, relationship, ownership, emotional or cognitive state. We achieve a "spiritual peace of mind." We begin the development of an emotional space within where the experience of calmness, tranquility, stillness, tenderness, gentleness, and a connection with one's divinity prevails. There is an experience of both transcendence of those energies that do not serve us and also transformation to some degree!

We achieve our passionate goals through spirituality and spiritual patience, perseverance, persistence, personal power, community support, and compassionate love.

No Boundary

As I open to Divine Energy.
Look right through to the truth in what I see.
For there is no boundary with Divine Energy.
Oh there is no boundary with Divine Energy.
No boundary.
No boundary.

As we open to Divine Energy
We look right through to the truth in what we see
For there is no boundary with Divine Energy
Oh there is no boundary with Divine Energy
No boundary.
No boundary.

Talk to
Look through
Merge into
Divine Energy

Yes, talk to
Look through
Merge into
Divine Energy

For there is no boundary with Divine Energy
Oh there is no boundary
With Divine Energy
No boundary
No boundary

For there is no boundary with Divine Energy
Oh there is no boundary with Divine Energy
No boundary
No boundary
No boundary
No boundary

© 2002 by Malaya Rider
All rights reserved.

Points to Ponder:

Are you conscious of your connection to your *chispa divina*?
What spiritual beliefs do you have that can aid you in your connection to and with *la chispa divina*?
What tools or methods could you use to connect with your radiant light within?
Could learning rebirthing (Reiki Tummo) serve your spiritual growth and development?
Would belonging to a spiritual community serve you and you it?

CHAPTER 10

Journeys Toward Essence

Close your eyes and imagine your intellect—all your cognitive thoughts—disappearing with all your defense mechanisms, beliefs, negative aspects of ego, socialization processes, judgments, and learned behavior. Now, with your eyes closed, imagine your feelings in your body reflective of your emotions disappearing with all the sadnesses, fears, and angers in all its depth, degree, intensity, and density within the emotional dimensions of time and space. Now, with your eyes closed, imagine your physical body with any pains or discomforts disappearing. Now, with your eyes closed, imagine your creative and intuitive abilities disappearing. Now, with your eyes still closed, imagine all your heart and soul centers disappearing. Now, with your eyes still closed, know that you are left with the eternal light of your spiritual infinite essence.

As I open to your presence
I can feel the "Essence"
My heart is shining with love
Beyond time.
As I open to your presence
I can feel the "Essence"
My heart is shining with love
Beyond time.
As I open to your presence
I can feel the "Essence"
My heart is shining with love
Beyond time.

With love
Beyond time
With love
Beyond time
Beyond time.

© 2002 by Malaya Rider
All rights reserved.

The Seven Spiritual Laws

La Jolla/UTC, California

The room was filled with spiritual seekers and those interested in raising their state of consciousness. People would come from a variety of states and countries in the world as well as locals from San Diego County. The companionship brought forth a sense of bonding and community and was always in a celebration of spirit. The participants present certainly helped to dissipate any loneliness that may have prevailed by those in attendance. It was another Monday evening in the suburb of San Diego known as La Jolla/ UTC. The residents of La Jolla thought of their unique city aside from San Diego. *La Jolla* is a Spanish word meaning the "the jewel"! Many tourists visit La Jolla because of its beauty that encompasses the sea and its coves, the village and the presence of its fashionable retail outlets, the highlands and their flowers, and street lined with palm trees.

We gathered every Monday evening, and the facilitator Ken would lead us initially in a loving mediation. His long thin body, full facial features, wavy hair, and voice echoed loving, low-keyed, earthy tones. He always seemed to radiate a sense of mellowed joy, harmony, and peace. The meditation would last approximately twenty minutes and then we would return our consciousness to the room. When our awareness once again became present introductions would ensue and a chapter from the *Seven Spiritual Laws of Success* by Dr. Chopra would be read.

The Chopra Center had closed shortly after the destruction of the Twin Towers in New York City, and Irene, the facilitator was kind enough to allow members of the group to congregate at her home for book discussions. Irene was an advocate of the Chopra Center and a leader in the spiritual community. She would share her spiritual journeys to India by way of word and photo presentation with the group.

Our goal was to raise spiritual consciousness in relationship to topics centered on Dr. Chopra's Book titled *The Seven Spiritual Laws of Success*. We were present to raise spiritually conscious questions based upon comments in the group. It was always a thrill for me and others to point out and expand upon aware and unaware contributions of thoughts and words in the book discussion!

Irene was the facilitator. She was a person who would place focus on the topics in the chapter of the book. She would always be bringing us back to the point in the chapter if and when participants became sidetracked. Today it was the law of karma. You know, cause and effect, "purpose." What is your purpose? What does that mean? Could it mean what was I brought here to accomplish? Could it mean for every action taken there is a reaction? For every bad thought I had would there ensue negative energy and for every good thought would there ensue positive energy? I guess it meant just that! Perhaps it meant more. I didn't know, but I knew my purpose. My purpose was to empower others by sharing my loving insight. This purpose was bestowed upon me as a result of doing personal growth work for two weeks in a group.

There were others in the room who shared their purpose as well. Jerry's purpose was to be happy and healthy. Elsa's purpose was to give and receive. Steve's purpose was to raise consciousness through electronics. Rodney's purpose was to raise maximum joy and harmony. Irene's purpose was to heal and transform self and others.

Eleanor-Frances's purpose was to do the kindest thing when in doubt, and Elaine's purpose was to be happy and enjoy life.

The topic for this evening's discussion was judgment. Jonathon was a participant who was committed in his conviction to be in judgment of others!

We agreed that it depended upon the type and nature of the judgment. We agreed that moral judgments could be made when an action or actions are practiced by a person or persons that are hurtful, traumatizing, painful, or deadly. Certainly it is inappropriate to commit genocide in the world.

A discussion would always ensue. The group would participate and make comments on the actualized topic or issue. Some participants would comment about judgment. Is it a spiritual judgment or was it a moral judgment or was it both? It seemed appropriate to make moral judgments in certain circumstances. It was appropriate to make a moral judgment when an individual or individuals practice genocide. Yes, it is so, and the group agreed with Jonathon!

When is a judgment detrimental? It is detrimental when the judgment is made because of one's belief system. The individual decides or reacts from his or her belief system that another's words or actions are wrong. It doesn't necessarily harm another person physically but emotionally a person can be impacted by the invalidation. Practicing unconditional love toward humankind helps to dissipate one's own beliefs. Practicing not taking what is said personally by the individual who the judgment is directed at is another way of responding to others' belief systems.

Rainbow Spirits in Lawson Valley

The nonnative, sacred, spiritual sweat lodge had moved from Poway, California, to Jamul, California, and it was my first journey to its new location. Jeff "Happy Bear" Goss lead the ceremonies at the new location in Lawson Valley. He had a vast background and experience over many years leading spiritual seekers on the path of the nonnative, sacred, ceremonial sweat lodge.

Here is how the journey to the sweat lodge unfolded. We entered Lawson Valley in San Diego County driving 5.5 miles around curving roads with the ridges of the surrounding hills peering down upon my bright red Mazda 626 LX. The beige stones protruded from the surrounding hills. The stones were spiritlike with a thousand eyes that seemed to be in constant observation of all movement of my small red vehicle with its single inhabitant. The early summer air was dry, clean, and invigorating to the spirit. However, the temperature was beginning to rise. The sense of peacefulness and tranquility was ever present. I spied my friend's vehicle ahead of me. Her green Honda and Montana license plate with black letters and towering Blue Mountain was easily recognizable from the California white and blue colors. I pulled alongside her vehicle and jesting to her said, "What is a Montana girl doing in Lawson Valley?" She seemed relieved upon glancing at me and said, "Gee, I'm lost and glad you're here to help me find the location of the sweat lodge."

I described to Danielle the spiritual significance of the nonnative American sweat lodge the day before and encouraged her to participant. She was searching for stability and anchoring. I had given her lessons in peer cocounseling, and she adapted to it quickly. She was hurting from loss of income in the ever-roller-coaster rides of the American stock market. Danielle had lost much money and was fighting periods of depression. She had hoped to have retired and experienced a state of relaxation by her fiftieth birthday. However, retirement was not to be experienced. Her stocks had taken a dramatic downturn, and her emotional body had experienced trauma. She was emotionally reeling from the market's ruthless schizophrenia. The bills from her other properties had started to pile up and overwhelm her emotionally. She had sought psychological help but had been somewhat frustrated by its slow paper processing. Her monotone and body posture was rigid, defensive, and lacked any animation. There was no joy or love or sense of pleasure. The emotion had been drained from her body. There was pall coldness about her demeanor. The exception was her dog! It was as fragile as she seemed to be. Shanti was a German shepherd who warmed up to Danielle in a kind and loving way. It was just what she needed. The shepherd had gentle warmth in its demeanor, and it was a tried and true companion! We had peer cocounseling and as is the habit when spirit is present animal life undergoes a transformation of silent presence or curiosity. The silent sound of the animal world when spirit is present is overwhelmingly loud and frozen, icy still! I have often mused on its contrast. But above all I have experienced its sense of knowing and its respect for spirits' presence. The animal world has a way of knowing when the invocation and evocation of spirit is taking its place!

Animals seem to experience its presence intuitively in an unexplainable and uncanny transparent vision in connection with creation itself! I have often found that humankind has ignored spirits' presence in similar circumstances when the animal world intuitively sensed spirit commanding an overpowering presence! It is truly an intuitive sense that the animal world instantaneously comprehends. It is a natural process for the members of its kingdom. Humankind is just too absorbed in its own head to have a similar awareness. Except for those special few who had practiced connection with the spirit and were in the spiritual power of the *now*!

It became very hot and dry this June day as we began to enter the valley. It was my first experience being in Lawson Valley. The roads were ever winding and could be treacherous at speeds greater than thirty-five miles an hour. Danielle followed me perhaps reluctantly but somehow with faith in me! The road ended, and we drove through a shadowed oak grove. It was cool in contrast to the heat of the valley. The oaks seemed ancient and dark and foreboding. It was as though they underwent a dark cloud and crucifixion. The oak grove was sinister for two strangers. Yet it was cool and refreshing. We just wanted to find the sweat lodge. The sky lost its blue canopy, and we continued through the darkness that surrounded us. Were we close to its location? I drove on and suddenly the grove ended, and we saw the sky once again! The heat was unbearable, but we continued along our way. The ridges along the road seemed formidable and impenetrable. We arrived at a fork in the road. There was a marker with the address we were seeking. We had arrived.

Several fire tenders greeted us at the sweat lodge location, and the facilitator was present. The lodge was much larger than any I had previously experienced. There were stockpiles of logs shaped in a half circle. It seemed like there were thousands of logs.

I commented to the fire tenders about the major human effort that must have contributed to the creation of the Lawson Valley nonnative, sacred, ceremonial sweat lodge. This sweat lodge was larger than the one in Poway, and many more participants were present. There are four rounds in the sweat lodge experience. The first one being gratitude and personal empowerment; the second, prayer for family, the Earth, and others; the third serves as a release of anything not serving our highest good; and the final round is visionary. During the sweat lodge experience itself many shared their spiritual traditions during the sacred calling forth of spirits for healing, health, abundance, and peace. The sweat lodge was a catalyst for all present to be in touch with their spiritual essence. I share a chapter about the nonnative, sacred, ceremonial sweat lodge experience in the book *I Dare to Heal with Compassionate Love.*

The nonnative, sacred, ceremonial sweat lodge has moved to Madre Grande in San Diego County. Locating information is in the resource section.

Pilgrimage to the World Trade Center, New York City

It's raining with mercy
It's raining with love
I am . . . that I am
I am that I am.

© 2001 by Inner Harmony Music
Words and Music by Michael Stillwater-Korns

Whispering spirits
In whispering winds
Whispers grace,
Whispers renewal
In a circle of love,
In a circle of peace
They are all one.

In memory of those who lost their lives at the
World Trade Center.

There was an old culture of systemic, structural, and legalistic rigidities that inhibited clear and decisive communication and action between governmental agencies. There was adequate fear and denial because of this environment among those individuals within governmental agencies that prevented transformation. It was this that prevented clarity and decisive action from taking place which contributed to the catastrophe of the destruction of the World Trade Center!

Comments from witnesses at the September 11 commission:

It was the middle of December just a couple of months after the World Trade Center was destroyed by terrorists, and I was to meet my friend Don Schmall that day near the site of the former Twin Towers for lunch. I hadn't seen him in several years, though we've been keeping in touch by phone and was looking forward to our reunion. Don is a tall man in his sixties who received a degree in engineering from Rensselaer Polytechnic Institute. I have never known him to say a negative word about any human being. Don is an activist and for people's health and well-being. I have always known him to be intelligent, caring, thoughtful, considerate, and passionate about the well-being of others. He is knowledgeable in the field of vitamins, minerals, and herbs and always responsive in a thoughtful and courteous manner when people approach him for advice. He is involved in several groups in the New York City metropolitan area providing information about the benefits of natural health and healing and working for a better national health system. He is a go-to individual when people seek alternatives to prescription drugs and advice about their illnesses. Don is also a skillful and intuitive peer cocounselor. We have counseled many times over the decades.

I approached ground zero after having lunch with Don Schmall and felt an immediate sense of grief at the magnitude of the tragedy that transpired at the site. I thought of those family members who were still in sheer grief of those who have lost their loved ones. I knew the key was for people to access their grief with listening support and negotiate their feelings. Again, this is a gradual process. The emotional impact of the bringing down of the Twin Towers at World Trade Center will be long lasting. The many lives that have been lost, the realization of vulnerability of the United States is yet to be realized. There are those individuals who have yet to realize their own impermanence and vulnerability in life. The shock is so great that denial permeates one's reality, awareness, and consciousness.

Humankind seemed frozen in an uncanny state of silence. The shock of disbelief just seemed to permeate the moment. The rain was coming down upon the narrow streets that bordered the former

WTC site. Broadway was near and vehicles lumbered along the streets on either side. The crowd was small, but the silence was overwhelming. The smell of jet fuel and its stench in the surrounding air was evident. We seemed to share and feel a range of emotions which naturally rise within us. Anger of great depth, degree, and dimension was present. The density and intensity of the feelings of those surrounding me was unknown to me, but I certainly sensed strong emotions and the emotional vibrations from a shared sense of disbelief of others who stood shoulder to shoulder with me. Sadness and grief with its overwhelming sensation was incomprehensible to the intellect. I could sense these emotions as they penetrated through the crowd. We were spiritually one with these feelings, feelings, feelings. There was no stopping them. They came naturally. The feelings were overwhelming, numbing, and paralyzing. We seemed paralyzed in time and space in the moment. There was a knowing of the horror that took place here. Here! Nearby!

The deceased spirits were there. I sensed the spirits who seemed to hold a vibration of denial. I felt their crying out of disbelief. I felt grief, and I sensed their grief as well! The tragedy was caught infinitely in their cries. It was in their horror of disbelief that transcended present time. It sent chills up and down my spine!

There were the spirits of the dead in states of horror declaring the sheer terror in the instant moment when there was nowhere to hide, to run. There was no safe haven, no safe and secure place around. I felt spirits in states of hysteria. It was an uncanny, eerie feeling that was ever present! I had awareness of deceased spirits that cried out their hopelessness and helplessness. There was a sense of an impending death coming. I had a sense of sheer nonacceptance of reality by those alive in the crowd and those who met their untimely death. They didn't want to accept it! There was a crying out for help in their total helplessness! There was no one to help! The situation was hopeless. It was truly terrifying to have these sensations. I can only perceive that others had similar horrifying thoughts and feelings.

I stood in the rain sensing the helplessness of these spirits. I stood in the rain sensing the horror of these spirits reaching out in desperation! The crowd seemed to humanly sense the plight of spirits shouting out in horror! The crowd just seemed to be humanly in touch with the spiritual essence of the deceased.

The Journey to Queretero

There were eighteen of us from the state of California. We were accepted to a program of study in the state of Queretero, Mexico. The state was located approximately forty-six hours from San Diego, California. I was reluctant to go because it was a new program, and it didn't seem like the program had been planned properly. I was correct in my perception. It was an opportunity to advance in the teaching profession and obtain a bilingual credential. I wasn't going to attend because it seemed like a program for those who already were fluent in the Spanish language. I went for an orientation, and the program coordinator claimed that the program would have three grammar levels. There would be an intermediate lower, intermediate upper, and advanced. She said that the intermediate lower could advance to the second half of the class. There would be two three-week sessions.

I knew it would be a challenging experience to adapt to studying in Mexico. I had experienced studying in Mexico before in the city of Ensenada. The city of Queretero was different. The city was deep into Mexico. This would be a world different from what I had ever experienced.

I was traveling alone to Tijuana, Mexico, from San Diego, California. A friend drove me to the Mission Valley Trolley Station. This was early in the morning for me, and it was difficult to carry the backpack from the house to the car. I thought I would get used to it. I started sweating as I lifted my backpack out of the car. The backpack was heavy and awkward. I haven't been backpacking in a long time.

The journey through Mission Valley on the trolley in early morning was wonderful. The hills on either side towered over the valley. The green hills were truly beautiful because of the winter and spring rains. It felt good to be leaving San Diego for a while and experience something new. I was truly happy to leave Mission Valley where I had lived for many years. I hadn't had a break from my job in a long time, and it felt good to get away. I had just found out a couple of days before that my part-time teaching job had ended. I felt disheartened. I felt discouraged but knew that my interest in employment lie in the field of psychology and teaching English as a Second Language. The English as a Second Language had been a useful job for I knew what my authentic calling had always been. My calling had been in the field of counseling / transpersonal psychology. I think teaching psychology would be an appropriate goal. I decided also to apply to the Marriage Family Therapist Program at the university.

The trolley ride lasted one hour. A young woman boarded the trolley in the downtown area. She was young, in her twenties, quite beautiful with black hair, dark eyes, and a very shapely figure. She claimed to have spent the night in a holding cell at the San Diego Police Station. She was an unhappy camper. She kept on wanting to tell her story over and over again. The story of how horrible it was to be in a holding cell and sleep on the floor with other women. She was anxious about her experience as she spoke about it in her mobile phone and anxiously caught the attention of others seated in the trolley car when she, in an animated way, spoke of her distressful experience. She looked tired but was young and sexy! That certainly drew the attention of other men on the trolley car.

We arrived at the border, and I disembarked from the trolley and walked across the San Ysidro border crossing. It was a quiet morning at the border mainly because it was early on Saturday. San Ysidro border crossing is a main thoroughfare for thousands of people arriving and leaving the United States and Mexico. It is an extremely active border with thousands of cars being inspected as they pass through the border.

Queretero, Mexico

I journeyed to the city of Queretero, Mexico. The city is known as "The Pillars." I like to think of the city as a pillar of sixteenth-century Spanish spirituality whereupon the other cities in the Mexican state of Queretero depend. It is the city of spiritual essence, the hub where other cities in the state of Queretero can look to as a source for culture, commerce, and inspiration. This city is a treasure of Catholic spirituality with churches in a variety of locations. The site of the city of Queretero was taken from the indigenous Indians by the Spanish in the 1500s. The Franciscans began establishing their presence in the form of missions and decided to domesticate the indigenous people. It was taken from the indigenous peoples in the 1500s when Hernan Cortez came to Mexico and conquered the natives.

The city is populated by one million Mexicans and has a colonial center with narrow cobble streets, cafes, plazas, picturesque windows that are examples of unique architecture in Latin America. It has a major town square where families and friends can congregate, clowns and musicians can entertain, and traditional Mexican music can be heard and enjoyed. The bustling activity of the city is interrupted by the occasional and sudden downpour of rain that soon dissipates into mild humidity. Children play in the streets, and vendors exhibit their wares competing for the tourist dinero. Beads, dolls, sandals, and souvenirs are displayed for purchase. The aromas of sumptuous Mexican foods fill the plazas and alleyways. There are plazas in the center of the city where people can meet and enjoy moderate temperatures as they relax from the stress of the day.

The Spiritual City of Bernal

The city of Bernal, approximately one hour from Queretero, draws many spiritual seekers. It is the "roca," the spiritual voice of God which permeates the surrounding countryside. The *roca* is a spiritual vortex and an attraction for residents and for those spiritual seekers who come for emotional and spiritual cleansing.

The huge rocklike pyramid shoots out of the earth and takes center stage in the village of Bernal. The "rock" is majestic in its overpowering presence in the village. It can be seen from any point in the surrounding countryside. Its form and shape is overwhelming and overpowering. Many people come from many places to experience its magnetic healing energies. It is the magnetism of the rock that brings forth the negative energies from the heart, the soul, the mind, the emotions, and the body. The roca is a spiritual vortex and an attraction for residents and for those spiritual seekers who come for emotional and spiritual cleansing. The result is a divine experience.

I journeyed to the city of Bernal and experienced the voice of spiritual essence and calling that invokes the natural healing that many believe comes about because of their visit. The residents and tourists complete their pilgrimage to the roca by climbing its circular cobblestone and dirt path to ascend to its apex. There are those who claim to have received enlightenment by climbing the winding cobble-and-rock-filled path.

The tourists and residents claim magical healing occurs because of their pilgrimage and homage to Bernal. They claim the roca is a catalyst that helps them connect with their spiritual essence.

The Women

I shared a very positive experience with my fellow students in the city of Queretero. We arrived in Queretero and seven of us were together in one house. There were four women in one room, two women in another room, and I had my own room. The women asked me the next day to move to my own room outside the main building so I agreed to accommodate them. I enjoyed being the only man with six women even though at times it became emotionally challenging to accommodate them. However, the women understood the difficulties a man might have being in the presence of seven women. They also accommodated me as well.

There were several Latin American women and two American women among the seven. It was here where I focused on staying connected to my spiritual essence. It enabled me to maintain patience and enabled me to respond to them rationally and prevented me to react in situations that were stressful. I maintained a positive attitude and relationship with the seven women throughout the one-month period in Queretero.

Jackie always had a positive attitude. She was always upbeat even when negative experiences occurred. She had Spanish-speaking parents and had lived in Puerto Rico previously. She practiced aikido—a martial art—to maintain her focus. Tammy was Anglo and already spoke excellent Spanish. She had lived a year in a Latin American country experiencing the trials of village life. Tammy was self-assured and was wonderfully upbeat and a positive person. She had a very strong and solid presence. She was quite intelligent. Patricia was from Northern California and grew up in the San Francisco area. She was light skinned and Latin American men seemed quite attracted to her. There were several women from Mexican families who were warm, outgoing, and very supportive. They were all very personable. I enjoyed their presence and celebrated life with them as we explored the cafes and restaurants of downtown Queretero in the old colony in the cool of the evening. We stayed together for a month's time and traveled to the Sierra Gorda where we visited a variety of monasteries and villages. The Sierra Gorda is a large mountain range in the state of Queretero. It is in this area where the rare stones of opals are mined. I had the fortune to stay with a young Mexican Cuban family. There was Miriam and Andreas who were both very warm and outgoing and their child, Emma Christina.

Points to Ponder:

Have you ever considered joining a book discussion group whose emphasis is on healing and spiritual growth?

Have you ever experienced the spiritual calling of the deceased?

Have you ever experienced a nonnative, sacred, ceremonial sweat lodge?

Have you visited places in the world that are said to be vortices of emotional cleansing and spiritual connection?

Are you connected to your spiritual essence?

Can you stay connected to your spiritual essence when you are confronted by stressful or distressful experiences?

Have you ever taken a class on how to meditate?

CHAPTER 11

The Cognitive Nuances
Our Cognitive Quotient
Some Advice

There are a variety of cognitive actions that we can take to acquire more depth, degree, and dimension in order to experience more spiritual power and enlightenment. We act to develop our cognitive quotient.

Significance of Choice

We can always make a cognitive choice even though we may feel emotional hurt in doing so. It's our well-being and happiness that we risk when we make choices that do not coincide with our nature. We learn quickly to differentiate between what choices are healthy for ourselves and what choices hurt us and create trauma for us in our lives. We learn this from our experiences.

There are certain choices that hurt us but are required by our situation or circumstances. This may be considered adult choices and may involve our taking responsibility for children. Children's needs come first before our own. This is a common and necessary choice that adults make. We take responsible actions and make responsible choices that result in our maturity. We use our personal growth tools and methods to get through our tensions that arise. We then experience greater depth in our cognitive faculties because of making mature and necessary right choices. We learn that family needs come first before our own. We mature because of our sacrifice. We have learned to give of ourselves.

We learn how to think and feel good about ourselves regardless of our sacrifices. Our nature may react against us. We can hurt within if and when we don't have the maturity to feel good about ourselves sacrificing for others. We learn to respond rationally to our environment.

Our choice to give can be tough on us in a practical, cognitive, emotional, and spiritual way. We can then proactively learn to act upon our attitude by invoking and maintaining the thought and affirmation of "it's time to take charge of our world" or "it's time to take charge of the world [meaning our own]."

We create tension within if and when our actions do not coincide with our natures. The surrender and release of our tensions manifests self and with patience comes integration of the above affirmation. We surrender and release feelings associated with tensions and the result is growth, integration, and maturity. If and when we experience fears, we learn to invoke our methods to take charge of ourselves as it relates to situations and circumstances. We then develop more spiritual/cognitive power, more enlightenment, and more emotional anchoring, and a stronger foundation within ourselves.

We take charge of our minds when our thoughts begin to race. This can occur if and when we begin to obsess about an issue in our lives. Many times we are focused on multiple tasks and our minds begin to speed up. We can lose control of our thoughts. We can lose control of our minds. We can then take charge of our worlds by saying the word "stop" to ourselves!

There is yet another choice. The choice of revealing our dark side whether it is through response or reaction or revealing our side endowed with grace, beauty, and understanding. There are times when I want to just tell people just the way I *feel* because of their reactions to me. I usually act by making a choice to respond in a sincere, direct, and graceful way. It works better.

We've met many who prejudge or misinterpret or are confused or have beliefs different from our own and their thinking differs dramatically. Their reactions and responses to us and situations are based on their beliefs and their experiences. Individual reactions and responses can vary greatly.

I've met many who are searching for a self-identity. They search for more of their self-identity. Why is it that we search? Why is it that we attempt to ignore the inner cravings and yearnings that bubble up from our suppressed and repressed feelings? The answer may lie in that it is our nature to nurture our nature infinitely.

We attempt to sedate the coming of the suppressed and repressed feelings but invariably what occurs is illness. The illness may take the form of a mental illness; for example, anxiety, depression, posttraumatic distress syndrome, asthma or other diseases. Our resistance to change, to transformation, to self-development can result in stress, distress, and disease. I believe these manifestations are wake-up calls from nature. They are the signs we need for our mental, emotional, spirit, spiritual, physical, social, and biological development. God wants us to manifest our cognitive, emotional, and spiritual power. God wants us to express our innate God-given calling and manifest it into the world. Our God-given calling serves to benefit ourselves and others.

We must use the ingredients of patience, perseverance, and persistence in our lives. Spontaneity can be positive, but rationality must always come first and must come within the perspective of long-term impact on ourselves and others. We can use the above affirmation to take charge of ourselves. This is an essential affirmation that we can use as a template for rational thoughts and can result in rational feelings. The thought—time to take charge of my world—helped me to seek out those thoughts and feelings that distracted me from nurturing my nature. The thought helped me to surrender and release feelings reflective of emotion that did not serve my nature and serve my calling in the world. The affirmation helped me to act!

This thought—taking charge of the world—helped me to observe those thoughts that came from both suppressed and repressed feelings. The thought set in motion my intuition and brought to me the realization of what disconnected thoughts and feelings as well as unhealthy thoughts and feelings impact me mentally.

The thought became a mirror of the distorted, disconnected parts of me that I needed to give attention to and address. The thought revealed to me the nuances of those dark shadows, gray areas, dark blotches reflective of the ranges of sadness to grief, anger to rage, and most important, of fear through terror. The thought helped me focus on unfulfilled tensions emanating from my frozen needs. The thought helped me to isolate and address with focus, effectively and efficiently, imprinted chronic distresses.

The thought helped me to focus on what I needed to surrender and release to become more of an integrated, whole, and healthy me. The thought helped me to be selective of what feelings required release. I was able to surrender and release feelings only if and when I was ready to do so both physiologically and psychologically. The thought prepared me for the emotional release process both mentally and physically. The thought helped me to focus on healthy thinking and feelings and right, healthy actions that required right intention on my part.

The thought was an enabling thought (motivated action) where intuitively I could perceive the depth, degree, the intensity and density of feelings, and emotional dimensions of my stress, distress, issues, and traumas. The thought gave me right prospective and right introspective of the inner workings of the dynamic components of the self.

Taking Responsibility for Ourselves

We are responsible to respond to ourselves. We take responsibility
by acting. Our actions reflect the ten components of our pyramid.
Once again they include: the mental, emotional, social, physical—
heart, soul, creative, spirit—and at our apex our spiritual.

The ten components each have their unique voice. The voice calls
out to us, and it is incumbent upon ourselves to respond to their
callings. We find that our distractions that block the callings sooner
or later just don't work.

Acquiring Specific and Accurate Details, Information, Knowledge, and Education

We use our tools and methods to clear emotion so that we better
develop and use our cognitive ability. We just think better. We
develop an investigative attitude with our cognitive abilities. We
determine specific, accurate details as it relates to acquiring specific
information. We acquire knowledge and education as it reflects
any issue we are addressing. We process our emotions so that our
empathy and compassion flourish. We assert ourselves to acquire
specific information. We integrate that information with our
previous information, knowledge and educate ourselves. We obtain
essential facts toward a spiritual solution to any specific issue
or set of issues. We use our tools/methods of healing, expansion,
evolution, and revolution so that we evaluate and reevaluate an
issue or issues regardless of the challenge or burden. This is a
circular process and leads us to a practical, spiritual solution
and is a direct link to our spiritual essence. The tools and
methods that resonate with us bring about our expansion,
evolution, revolution and result in enabling ourselves to respond
rather than react in any situation. We integrate our experience
emotionally, mentally, socially, etc., raise our consciousness and
respond and act with more spiritual power and bring more
enlightenment and wholeness to ourselves.

We learn to create and integrate an authentic self. We are able to respond and express ourselves rationally in the world. If, for example, the repair shop has failed to repair our automobile, we need to acquire the information, the facts, and the knowledge and educate ourselves about our automobile.

We assert ourselves with those in question and learn the principles of investigation to obtain the truth! We determine whether or not the repair shop is responsible or is it a defect in the car? I gathered my evidence and brought my auto issue into small claims court and won. The auto mechanic reimbursed me significant monies.

Positive Thoughts

We put focus on positive thoughts in our healing goal. Depending upon the depth, degree, nuances, and emotional dimensions of the suppressed and repressed emotional feelings, it can be an arduous task to place focus on positive thoughts. However, there cannot be any productive healing without positive thoughts. Thoughts have their own depths, degrees, dimensions, and nuances as do feelings. It is here where our cognitive quotient can be determined. It is determined by the cognitive attention we bring into the world.

Existing hurt and trauma feelings have a tendency to move a human being into a negative thought pattern. The reactions we have are dependent upon our psychosocial, economic, genetic, biological, environmental, and developmental makeup. They depend upon situations and circumstances that occur in our lives and those feelings that result in the way and ways we react to them. It's not always simple or easy to obtain clarity about a situation when our feelings are involved. This is the reason why it's important to have emotional clearing tools, techniques that resonate with us. Responding with objectivity and not reacting with subjectivity becomes our mission. We go for our emotional clearing.

Individual's New Individual Thought

Our spiritual power and enlightenment can include a new and individual thought. It's a thought that has never been thought before. The thought can create a greater realization of oneself. The thought can unfold into an awakening of consciousness that manifests itself into a new idea. The thought can emanate from one's continual connection with our divine spark. The divine spark is quite vocal once one has connected with it. It endows a being with a sense of eternal light, love, illumination, pathways to abundance, clarity, purity of emotion, and spiritual joy. The divine spark bubbles up in our intuition, emotions, spirit, spirituality, body, soul, heart, intellect, social relationships, creativity, and expands and evolves with our work and action.

Our Thoughts, Feelings
Others' Thoughts, Feelings

We can be impacted and/or triggered by others' thoughts, feelings, body languages, actions, or reactions. This is regardless to whether or not our perceptions are correct. We can be sensitive to the vibrations of how our own thoughts and others' thoughts impact/trigger our emotions. We can decide not to take on and absorb others' situations and circumstances. Children naturally take things personally! We must recognize that in doing so we take on emotional hurt. We are triggered! What is the range of our sadness, anger, and fear that result after something is said because of some dialogue, because of a situation or circumstance? What are our reactions and our behavior that results from the dialogue, situation or circumstance? Are we strong enough within to respond in a proactive, loving way or do we sink into reacting with anger?

Observing Those Thoughts that Do Not Nurture Your Nature and Your Reaction-Action-Reaction to Them

We all have situations and circumstances in our life that challenge our faith. We have situations that impact and trigger our present feelings—suppressed and repressed. The power of the situation and circumstances can trigger our distress patterns. Personal observation of our reaction and then acting to stay focused and negotiate our thoughts and feelings call forth how we experience a reaction. We can only choose if and when we allow and trust our intuition to flourish and are quick to observe our thoughts.

I was invited to a party by an acquaintance. I phoned her and claimed I was uncomfortable with some of the people who would be attending the party. She reacted with immediate anger. I returned her phone call and claimed she was rude and intrusive. She responded in a vicious way. I didn't immediately respond to her verbal deluge but felt anger. I used my methods/tools to surrender and release my feelings. I was able to act civil with her upon meeting her again. I didn't react. She gazed at me and responded that she had moved on from her emotional anger. I felt anger on subsequent occasions upon seeing her but continued to use my tools to surrender and release my feelings until I was able to transform my thinking. I was proactive in my relationship with me. It enabled me to create a neutral state in the relationship. I subsequently succeeded at relinquishing all negative energy regarding her. I experienced true forgiveness.

We Need to Make the Thought Adjustments

HALT

A conversation with a friend claims that the organization Alcohol Anonymous uses an acronym HALT. She believes that halt stands for Hungry, Angry, Alone, Lonely, and Tired. She claimed the acronym helps us to calm down instead of reacting and helps us to respond. HALT helps us to respond and refrain from reacting in situations.

I choose from a variety of psychological methods to make adjustments in my thinking. I use right intention to make and take right actions, transform my thoughts, and nurture my nature. I address the emotional body in order to successfully transform my thoughts. I recognize the significance of my emotions in conjunction with my thoughts.

When we are in tune with our emotional, heart, soul, physical and other bodies intuitively, we know exactly what thoughts are necessary to help us help ourselves connect emotionally with the energy of pain. We can then begin the direct process of emoting what is necessary by whatever tool or method we have at hand dependent upon what has either triggered the chronic, intermittent, or current stress or distress. This is reflective of present circumstances or situation.

Positive Attitude

The positive attitude comes from one's positive thoughts regardless of one's present situation. We take action to focus on positive thoughts and those thoughts impact our feelings which can impact our body language and emotional tone. The emotional tone reflects the sound of our words in the world. Do we speak from dissonance or are our words resonating with others? The words and body language impact the people around us and our environment.

Points to Ponder:

How aware (conscious) are you of your thoughts?
What is your awareness of what is said to you and its impact upon you?
How are you impacted emotionally from the negative news on radio, TV? What is your awareness of its impact upon you?
What is your cognitive quotient?
What are your reactions in situations beyond your control?

CHAPTER 12

Relationships

Relationship Consciousness

I love him because he seems to take and make the time and create a safe space for me so that he can listen to the nuances of my thoughts and my feelings.

—Said by a woman
about her man

As we see ourselves as beloved, we see others as beloved.

—Reverend Kevin Bucy, MDiv.
Religious Science Minister

Significance of Relationships Both Intimate and Others

Humankind has a need for a significant other. Nature calls on us to seek out and find *that* person. We have a need for that human connection. We are pilgrims who continue to look for *the one* who will *really* be there for us and listen! When that rational need is not being filled, it's painful, it hurts. The pain is stored in our emotional body and creates depression and anxiety. This is why we never stop looking for that *special* individual. This is a basic and a natural human need.

If we seek a significant other to fill an irrational emotional need, a hurt, a trauma, then our disappointment sooner or later will ensue. It is incumbent on us to respond and do our own emotional inner work. We make our own selves happy in doing so. We can then seek out another person to experience happiness and joy.

What is the consciousness of your significant other? What is your partner's lifestyle? Do you both have the ability to integrate your lifestyles and blend its nuances into your tapestry of love? I've learned the importance of determining and being sensitive to the wants, desires, and rational needs of a partner. I've also learned the importance of consciousness and alertness and awareness of and to irrational partner needs! Are both partners willing to support each other in resolving irrational needs? This is a key question that can bring greater joy, love, bliss, and peace to the relationship or it could bring stress and conflict. Do the partners put up or create walls?

Relationships work when both parties work with themselves effectively, efficiently, and with focus. Relationships work well when both parties are on "the same page." Our consciousnesses need to be in peace and not in pieces. When two people are of a similar consciousness then the relationship is in peace. When two people are not on the same page then the relationship may be in pieces. When two people are supportive of each others' expansion, evolution, and revolution, then the individuals can create a divine relationship in tune with each others nature. They create the power of spiritual oneness. We can develop a relationship if and when both partners work at, are willing, show a willingness to blend their lives nuances into a partner lifestyle.

Jim and Joyce

I have a friend Jim who told me this story about his relationship with Joyce. I've known Jim for twenty years, and he has practiced many holistic methods. Jim met Joyce and would confide in me about their relationship. He gave me permission to tell his story.

I met Joyce through a friend, and we took an immediate interest in each other. We became friends and dated each other for a brief time of three months. Joyce was from the southeast and spoke with a wonderful southeastern Dixie dialect. Joyce was slim, short, with black hair, and with unusually beautiful turquoise eyes. She would look great in her red skirt and burgundy pullover. She liked those red lipsticks that always seem to smear her lower lip. She would always be repeating the words "How are you, kid?" Joyce was intelligent in her own way.

She was jaded by the early passing of her mom and dad. She learned at an early age to take her own responsibility. It had to be hard for her to nurture herself at a young age. She was definitely a business woman who always was looking to make a deal. Selling was her life. She lived in the fast lane. She lived her life in an unconscious way. I determined after three months that we certainly weren't on the same page. I was disappointed because I liked her.

Many people have their preferences. It's best to tell one's truth from the beginning. When she told me that she wanted to date others after we've been intimate I explained to her that I just wasn't going to make an emotional investment of capital in a relationship with her and certainly didn't want to be exposed to sexually transmitted diseases. She didn't seem interested in a partner relationship at all! She claimed that it was wonderful being together but that for her it was a mistake. The realization came as a complete surprise.

I determined intuitively perhaps that she wasn't really interested in developing an authentic relationship with me. The woman did not reveal to me her truth. She was interested in being with a partner and earning so-called big money! Perhaps she was confused.

Perhaps she was in emotional transition or transformation and just needed a friend during this period of time. Our wants and needs were different. She was transitioning to dating again. She claimed to have resisted relationship for a long time. I thought she was ready to settle down after experiencing two traumatizing divorces. She had an emotional need to fill. I decided that I was not here on earth to fill her irrational emotional needs. When I said no to fulfill her needs and took charge she responded by saying "Let's be friends."

I trusted my intuition regarding her relationship intentions and was proactive by asserting myself with her. I choose not to participate in her irresponsible behavior. I would not buy into fulfilling her needs and "be her friend." I took charge and stated my own wants, desires, and needs. Her actions were confusing. I realized that I had been victimized, but that I was not a victim. Her mixed messages, behavior were self-centered. She just seemed to need a supportive male friend to get through her period of transition. She admitted to me that she had resisted relationship. She claimed a lack of intimacy with anyone over a long extended period of time. Was she telling her truth or was she confused?

I was disappointed but chose not to feel sorry for myself. I negotiated my feelings through a variety of methods and tools at my resource and experienced forgiveness of her and forgiveness within and of myself. I needed that forgiveness of myself because of my self-guilt because I was hurt! I felt guilt within because of an internalized self-judgment. I had internalized the thought "I should have known better." Using the word "should" cause self-judgment. This was an opportunity for me to learn self-forgiveness. I was hard on myself. I didn't realize sooner her needs. I was a man helping in Joyce's transition. I was a man who was there for her to fill her emotional needs during her transition. I was an in-between man to be there for her during her transformation. I was a secure anchor while she was going through her turmoil. However, I chose not to continue the rescue mission!

I needed now to experience self-love. I needed emotional healing to occur. I needed to release my anger and my sadness. My emotional healing, surrender, and release resulted in forgiveness. I forgive her as well. I was proactive in addressing my feelings, and this helped me to transform my hurt, darkness, and shadows into emotional light. I transformed the hurt into self-love and love for her. I was able to see the darkness in my eyes' transition into light in the reflection of my mirror. The process was a divine one. I integrated, expanded, and evolved more of myself. This was a natural progression. I succeeded in emotionally releasing the feelings reflective of my hurt emotions and reintegrated the experience as a memory. The personal and spiritual growth came as a result.

When I experienced enough emotional release, my inner peace returned. There was a spiritual peace as well. There was a spiritual connection that occurred. The darkness and the shadows dissipated, disintegrated, and my heart felt much lighter, and my soul felt cleansed. I felt more ordered and whole. I reconnected with my spiritual power.

I learned that it's important to ask many questions and to take one's time in getting to know another human being. I learned that intuition and emotion in getting to know someone is not enough.

Reflections of the Relationship of Jim and Joyce

When we have an aware, loving significant other in our lives it is a sure enabling power and it is a sure catalyst for healing many emotional issues and enhances the healing of physical issues as well. We have an opportunity to support our partner in their healing of their issues, their growth, evolution, and expansion as they have an opportunity to support us in ours.

There must be willingness on the part of both parties to do their inner work and aid in the healing work and evolution of each other in all facets of self. There must be effective communication between the partners so that both partners are alert and aware of each other. I have found it a challenge to find a partner who is open and expresses a consistent willingness to grow. The relationship is truly intimate when we can connect with a partner who has experience doing and achieving enlightenment. We seek a partner who expresses a willingness to initiate a spiritual level of commitment in relationship.

Partners begin in a gradual way to explore their cognitive, emotional, spiritual bodies and mature within themselves as they succeed with focus, effectiveness, and efficiency within. We create the quality of emotional time and create and make a quality space to be there for each other. When we are proactive and create enough quality time and space then the process of enhancing our divine personal power and enlightening our consciousness leads to a growing intimacy. This aids in our transformation, and together as a couple we expand and evolve.

When partners are in sync then they can work with focus effectively and efficiently with each other on their issues. When a partner reacts irrationally, the other can maintain a loving attitude by being there in an alert and aware manner. We can smile at them, make them aware of their unconsciousness, and love them for who they really are!

We take responsibility by paying attention to each others' thoughts, feelings, and create a listening space for each other to share needs. Succeeding at this usually takes work and depends upon the core beliefs and issues involved.

It requires training as well. It is here where a consciousness-raising, intimate, loving relationship creature comes into being. It is here where authentic intimacy expands, evolves, and matures with the partners and within each individual. This is a mutual relationship where both partners must get their individual needs met. The individuals must take the responsibility to be present for each other in an alert, aware, compassionate, empathetic, and loving way.

We have an opportunity to be there for each other when stresses and irritations arise in a relationship. Our awareness and honesty are essential. We must have the courage to show and experience our emotional vulnerability to ourselves and with our partner. It is a thing called trust. We develop trust within and bring it into the relationship with the other. We must learn to do our inner work and explore our feelings to succeed.

When we have become accustomed to succeeding with ourselves and doing our inner work, we very quickly discover that it's a great frontier, and we begin to learn the adventure of self-exploration and self-discovery. The self-exploration then becomes our thrill of awakening! This requires persistent, persevering, and patient practice and self-training. It also becomes fun as we learn to nurture our individual growth.

We can succeed at resolving our issues because of our inner intimate relationship. If and when we can make it happen for ourselves, then we can honestly say we have a conscious, consciousness-raising, enlightening, and spiritually empowering relationship. We can then say that our relationship is an authentic, intimate, and loving one. This is certainly ideal, but with tender loving care it's more than probable it is possible.

We develop an attitude of mutual cooperation. We develop an attitude of mutual giving and receiving. We develop a cooperative process that we bring into the relationship. I believe patience with ourselves and each other is a significant quality that we must bring into the relationship. We can learn patience. Our persistence and perseverance are two additional important qualities. We can then say that our emotional needs in a relationship can be met.

The Five Cs of a Relationship

We attempt to refrain from changing, correcting, criticizing, and controlling the other in relationship. We need to work with ourselves on these Cs.

We can suggest. We can begin with the word "I" and state that we are uncomfortable with the behavior of the other, *but* we cannot attempt to change, correct, control, or criticize the other. We can say "I feel sad about this behavior" or "I feel angry about this behavior" or "I feel afraid regarding this behavior." It's always incumbent upon the other to learn how to listen to the feelings of their partner. This lends to a healthy discourse and to compromise. We can also begin with the cognitive approach and say "May I suggest that _____." I believe that it's necessary to use both methods to dissipate conflicts in relationship. The key is that both partners express a willingness to participate.

It is here where the fifth *C* of compromise plays a significant roll. Compromise can be made easier when both individuals have experience or "act with willingness" to practice relationship methods. I like mirror work where both individuals listen to and repeat what is said to the one who has spoken. We learn patience, empathy, compassion; our flexible intelligence participates. We learn to reflect on the individual's hurts, traumas, and beliefs. We learn the reasons why individuals think, act, and behave the way they do. We learn about each others' beliefs based upon the individual's genetic, biological, developmental, and environmental experience. Practicing this method permits and allows us to raise our consciousness and permits and allows compromise. We can then learn to compromise in an empathetic and human way. We can then feel good about our compromising. The relationship expands, evolves, and we develop a better understanding for each others' experience. We can then learn to love each other in a more compassionate way.

We can use other methods as well to enhance our relationships and implement ways we can negotiate our three most difficult emotions and their reflective feelings in our bodies.

It's best not to have expectations in a relationship. It's best to discuss our expectations if and when we have them. Discussion opens the door and is another key to raising the consciousness of the relationship and learning compromise in situations where conflicts may arise. However, I have found discussion to be just not enough. Individuals must have other tools and methods to negotiate issues and conflict before satisfaction within and of the partners can be experienced. The reason being is that one's needs and emotions keep coming up!

Loss

Circular connected breathing is a magnificent tool to handle the suppressed and repressed feelings of loss. Loss of a loving relationship with a significant other, a child, a friend, a loved one, a job, a home, a pet, and whatever one can possibly think of. It is a tool that can truly help one make rational, logical sense out of nonsense. It can help one seek out, reevaluate, and get clear on hurt emotional feelings. These or those feelings get in the way of our being clear. The methods bring clarity to a confusing hurtful and painful situation.

Forgiveness and loss can go hand in hand. I feel the sadness, anger, and fear of a loss, loss of a loved one in death or loss of a loving relationship. I'm angry that the person left, passed away. I feel insecure at their passing, but with persistent, unyielding surrender and release of emotion, I experience rebirth. I move from my sense of loss to a sense of renewal. I experience a divine connection with my spirit and their spirit. I can transform loss into bliss, joy, harmony, peace, and happiness. I can move from a sense of grief to meaningful closure with a loved one. I can do a transition into the light and remove the darkness. The keys are many: not giving up, having faith, persevering through the emotional pain until it dissipates, and then moving on with our lives. Loss is an emotion shared by many who lost loved ones in the World Trade Center attack and those who have lost loved ones in the war in Iraq and Afghanistan.

Detachment

To be able to master detachment, one needs to practice. We can learn to detach emotionally from each others' pain energy and be there for each other in an empathetic and compassionate way. We can accomplish detachment with our significant other, family members, friends, and with other relationships.

Humankind can feel when we are there for them in an empathetic and detached way. Humankind can feel our presence when we are in close contact with them. The peer counseling method is an excellent modality where one can learn detachment. It's here where we can effectively learn to be there for others without becoming emotionally involved about their story.

Learning detachment and maintaining an empathetic concern for those who have been impacted—when hearing terrible news reports on TV and radio—is healthy for ourselves.

We can learn detachment for ourselves as well. We embrace the range of our human experience. This includes our past history. We experience our past history, our dips, bumps, potholes, craters, our stress, distress, our emotional hurts, our emotional traumas. We then can decide to transcend the pain and raise our energy to embrace our joy, bliss, and life force energy! We elevate our spirit with the divine one and view our soul in its innocence and essence. Then we can experience complete detachment with compassion and love for our own emotional and physical pain. Here again we can learn detachment from our emotional and physical pain and learn to transcend it and connect with divine energy. We can embrace our feelings of sadness, anger, and fear in relationship to any of our issues and decide to raise our vibration. Meditation is a wonderful tool to accomplish this purpose.

We can learn detachment from any stated goal. The key is to begin to learn to stay consciously present in the moment. We can learn to focus on being in the joy, bliss, peace, tranquility while taking any action. When we succeed at being in the moment then we can detach from any outcome. In the book *The Science of Mind*, Ernest Holm, the author and the power behind the "Science of Mind Movement," claims that detachment is wanting and desiring a goal or purpose without having the attachment to the result. We can be in the light as long as we have the capacity to breathe in the faith.

Points to Ponder:

What is the consciousness of your significant other? Do you have the courage to engage in authenticity in relationship?

Are you willing to express vulnerability and deepen your trust with your significant other?

Are you aware of each others' wants, desires, and needs?

Are you presently in a relationship?

Do you have an intimate relationship based upon being there for each other, listening in an animated manner?

Are you both doing your inner work in an effective, focused, and efficient way?

Is your love growing authentically as you both expand and evolve individually?

Do you both have methods and tools as resources to go to in order for both of you to do your individual inner work?

Are you patient, persistent, and persevering for your selves and supportive of each other?

Are you willing to acquire support from others if necessary?

Are you willing to practice the five Cs of relationship?

Are you up for the challenge of learning detachment?

CHAPTER 13

The Intuitive Nuances

There are people who place greater trust in
dreams, visions, and other heightened states of
emotion!

—William Blake
Vision and Dreams

There is a third eye or the brow chakra. It's here where we develop the depth, degree, and dimensions of perception, clairvoyance, and extrasensory perception. It's the energy that is focused on serving mankind and gives energy to those who seek beauty, love, and justice. This is the body that allows you to draw into inner peace, quiet, freedom, and to stretch boundaries. The thyroid/throat chakra also impacts the third eye by way of the cognitive and emotional components and by the expansion of our intuition.

Inspiration

The chakra of inspiration is said to be located at the third eye, on the forehead. This is said to be the gateway to the higher self. Included in the word "inspiration" is the spirit of the seeker. It is the "in spire," the "in breath," the "taking in of the breath" through the mouth or nose that enables the connection between mind and body! It is here where the individual seeks the wisdom that can be gained in the belief of a higher power that motivates us to go beyond our limitations.

Journey to Phoenix

I've never been politically active in my life. However, I had begun listening to C-Span TV and became inspired by listening to the candidates for president of the United States. C-Span TV is paid for by the cable network and is an asset for those interested in politics and authors.

I have always felt President Bush to be a good man but lacked flexible thinking and the depth of wisdom that only tested experience could bring. I intuitively felt that General Wesley Clark was the only candidate with the experience and wisdom to be the president of the United States. I've been listening to the Democratic candidates for president and became inspired by his flexible thinking, wisdom, and experience. I was also impressed by his wife. The primary election for Democratic candidates was being held in Phoenix, Arizona, and I felt motivated to join his campaign in the presidential primaries. I was reluctant to drive alone through the desert from San Diego, California, to Phoenix, but my intuition inspired and motivated me to do so. I had to put aside my doubts and fears of traveling alone through San Diego County and the Arizona Desert at night and arrive in Phoenix, Arizona, without knowing anyone. I had intention!

I phoned ahead from San Diego and spoke with several people at the Phoenix, Arizona, headquarters of General Clark and listened to Gert Clark, the general's wife make a presentation in Florence, North Carolina. I decided to feel through my fears and focus on the adventure of the unknown. I concluded that Phoenix, Arizona, was my destination that very day. I decided to stretch my boundaries and go beyond my limits and go with my intuition and faith. I went for it and got involved in politics!

I enjoyed the drive through the desert stopping at Dateland and devouring a famous date shake that was just heavenly. I loved the quiet of the desert and enjoyed the scenery of the Mohawk Valley known as an agricultural center, and Painted Rock, known for its petroglyphs art work.

I arrived in Phoenix without a map and asked directions from people on the street for the location of the Clark campaign headquarters. I certainly had my fears, but my intuition enabled me to maintain my faith and my emotional stability enabled me to think clearly and follow directions. I arrived at the Clark campaign headquarters and met the manager. He seemed surprised when I told him I had come alone from San Diego on my own initiative to support and volunteer for the Clark campaign. He made a phone call and found a place for me to stay.

I located the residence early Sunday morning and met Daniel and Helen for the first time in my life. They welcomed me as a new friend with much warmth. I sat down at their table and noticed a Star of David on their kitchen wall. I had a sense that an angel spirit and faith had guided me to Phoenix, Arizona. Daniel and Helen accommodated me with my own room for four nights. They were wonderful new friends. I participated in the Wes Clark campaign for the next four days canvassing, cold calling, and doing visibility in Phoenix.

I went on TV and radio in English and Spanish the night of the primary election and had an opportunity to come face to face with the governor of Arizona. I certainly let go and let God in. I felt the spirit move me to act and allowed and permitted myself to do so. I didn't allow fear, doubt, or reservation to take charge of my wanting, desiring, and needing to act in the best interests of myself and others. I went beyond my boundaries and limitations and got involved politically!

Colorful Burnt Bun Café

I intuitively decided to travel a different route home sensing that undiscovered experiences lay on my journey. I was not disappointed.

I left Phoenix the day after the primary elections and drove through the desert. The Burnt Bun Café is a white one-story building with a bright-red-painted, two-foot stripe surrounding its top. The letters of the Burnt Bun Café are painted in red. It lies at the crossroads of Highway 347 South and Highway Arizona 84 just twenty or so miles south of Phoenix. I arrived at the café midmorning to find a group of senior-aged bikers with their Harley Davidson Choppers congregating just outside. They were preoccupied with discussion and well nourished after a hearty morning breakfast. They were wearing the traditional black jackets, leather jeans, chains attached to their black wallets, and scarves around the tops of their heads. The other bikers wore their peak black hats. There was a high blue sky with few clouds hovering above as I walked through the main door. I entered the restroom and was confronted by a sign over the john that read in bold letters "Please hold down the handle and keep the restroom clean because your mom is not here to clean up after you." After leaving the restroom I entered the main dining room. There was an elderly gentleman seated at the far end of the table gossiping with one of the female workers about the daily happenings around town. I loved their southern dialect. It was down to earth and unpretentious. I thought I had walked into a Hollywood stage set with an abundance of character actors. However, this was the real thing. A waitress whose name was Betsy blurted out in no uncertain terms to the biker seated at the counter how he deserved a piece of his hide removed because of his inappropriate upbringing. I ordered a cup of tea with lemon, and the biker seated at the counter began a discussion about the nasty weather in Northwestern Pennsylvania. This was the beginning of February, and the cold weather prevailed back east. The nasty weather had brought the biker to settle in this rural out-of-the-way desert town. This whole experience was startling for me since it was totally unexpected and was like a scene from Marlin Brando's old films or a Rod Sterling half-hour *Twilight Zone* episode. I paid for my cup of tea and decided it was time to leave the Burnt Bun Café and continue on my journey home to San Diego.

Visualization and Visioning

I believe that both visualizing and visioning are components of and intuitive sense of being. I define these words as follows:

Visualizing: We can visualize resolving many issues in our lives. If we have a health problem we can visualize our healing. We can see it take form and shape in reality in our everyday life. We can visualize both our physical and emotional well-being in the world. We can visualize accepting wellness in our lives. The acceptance of our wellness in our mind-body connection contradicts our pain and functions to help us surrender and release our feelings reflective of the emotions. The cognitive visualization can help us help ourselves negotiate the pain. Above all we must be proactive and take practical steps and embark upon our healing process. Success is not in all ways guaranteed, but we must commit ourselves to achieving our goal. This is why visioning is essential.

Visioning: It can be an agenda, an opinion or it can be a purpose in our lives. We use our intuition in order to help us help ourselves determine the other steps into reclaiming our well-being, divine personal power, and our enlightenment. We accomplish a greater depth, degree, and dimension of our connection to the divine spark within. It is our essential goal to reconnect with our divine essence. We can better live with pain in our body when we achieve the connection with our spiritual power. We acquire resolution of unhealthy debilitating energy by using our intuition. We inquire of others the names of competent practitioners who have the knowledge and skill to resolve our issues. I resolved my back pain by finding a competent shiatsu therapist. She performed Japanese massage.

Points to Ponder:

Do you have enough faith and daring to join a political campaign in another state?

Are you willing to go beyond your boundaries and limitations by developing and expanding your intuitive skills?

Do you use your intuitive abilities with your family, friends, employment, and recreational activities?

Do you ever visualize well-being in your life when challenged by health issues?

CHAPTER 14

Our Soul Nuances

Spirit-Soul

We nourish ourselves by invoking the breath of spirit so we experience a cleansing of those feelings that do not serve us in our body. These are feelings which are reflective of our unhealthy emotions. The cleansing of our unhealthy emotions nourishes our soul and endows us with self-love! It leads to a state of bliss synonymous with our authenticity. We are then human beings who are becoming whole and experiencing our holiness.

We must be proactive when we are restrained by emotional knots and distress. We use methods that resonate with ourselves, i.e., emotional release, meditation, martial arts to free and to liberate our spirits. We are then nourishing our souls. Our souls then begin to *free* themselves from those unhealthy emotional burdens that bind them.

We free more of our emotional body by doing good deeds, prayer, and participate and obtain group support. We use those tools/ methods that resonate with ourselves to free more of our spirits from shadow and the darkness. We learn to work efficiently, effectively, and with focus and free more of our souls to dwell in infinite peace. This is an ongoing process always resulting in a rising of consciousness and freeing more of our innate flexible intelligence. We endow our spirit with spiritual divinity and free more of our infinite soul to experience harmony!

Developing an "Inner Sense" of the Infinite Soul

The catalyst of the connected breath enables us to go into, surrender, and release feelings reflective of emotion that doesn't serve us. It enables us to expand and evolve the components of self, i.e., the mental, emotional, spiritual, physical, and social. When we use the circular, connected, healing breath it enables us to open our hearts and therefore invoke love without limits. The breath helps us to hold an intention of connecting with our spirit and our spirit connecting with a universal power! I believe "universe" means but one ongoing "uni-verse" or a unification of the self into whole and holiness.

The thread becomes a conduit growing ever larger within, creating more emotional in spiritual time and space. Therefore, we have a sense of elevating spirit expanding and evolving our relationship to the universal one. It becomes the key that unlocks the door to love, expanding and evolving and experiencing its purity. We deepen our sense of love in infinite time and space. There is an invocation and an evocation of soul. It continues on its journey of expansion and evolution. It becomes eternal. Creation is at work! Soul journey invokes peace, joy, and love.

When we become sophisticated in using methods and tools that resonate with us we can have a soulful outer body experience. We can sense our soul afloat. We can look inward and observe our soul timeless in space. We can view the soul by closing our eyes and observing it within with clarity. Please go ahead and do that now!

There is also a sense of infinite peace that prevails. Peace prevails when we have achieved harmony of mind, body, spirit, and soul. There are no boundaries. Time and space become seamless, expand, and evolve. There are colors of the rainbow in texture and form. The rainbow colors ever expand and fill our inner consciousness with peace of mind, tranquility, purpose, and right action!

We develop the emotional depth, degree, dimension, and most importantly, resiliency to open our hearts more and more, invoking love and elevating our own spirit by way of the catalyst of the divine breath. The breath is the key component in connecting with the divine spirit! The connection with the divine spirit facilitates opening the door to viewing the purity of the soul. When we become experienced using circular breath methods we can reconnect with our spiritual power quickly. We experience an immediate recharging of our batteries.

Points to Ponder:

Are you connected to your soulful body?
What do you do to nurture your soulful self?

CHAPTER 15

The Physical Nuances

The use of movement in any form opens a door to the emotional body: addresses tensions, begins to address emotional blocks, helps to relax us, and facilitates release of feelings associated with stress or distress.

Exercise

Exercise is important to the physical body's health. It's not enough to release the feelings associated with the distresses. I've met many people who conclude that exercise is great but is not enough to negotiate all feelings reflective of unhealthy emotions. Exercise may be enough for most stress experiences on a daily basis but certainly not enough to address deep-seated, implanted, ingrained, distressing, and traumatizing feelings. I've heard the comment of "I've run ten miles today; however, I still do not feel that was enough to dislodge the deep-seated tension I'm feeling."

Some suppressed emotion is released through exercise, but the levels of feelings associated with hurt and distress reflect a myriad of nuances in depth, degree, and dimension. When I speak about dimension I refer to the emotional hurt that occupies emotional time and space that takes our attention. It reduces our awareness of the world. The hurt blocks our spacious free attention, restricts, reduces, and impacts the degree and amount of our alertness and awareness in the world. We aren't as happy as we were before the hurt experience. We feel weighed down by the excess baggage.

I have a friend named Tim who swears by bicycling. It's his passion. I believe he rides his bike several times each week. It's great weight control and helps to release tension from his work and relationships! Sports are great for daily stress but are certainly not sufficient for ingrained, deep-seated feelings. My friend subsequently notified me of his heart attack. He claimed that stress was the cause of his illness. I was willing to help Tim address his deep-seated distress but he refused.

Dance

I love to dance to the melodies of country, Western music. One can connect to both the beat and the rhythms through dance. Every cell in one's body comes alive. We can experience true freedom in movement and become in tune with the harmonies of the music. The ideal dance is when we become freed up of self-consciousness and our bodies harmonize in movement with the beat and rhythms of sound. Dancing is relaxing and is a door opener for many people. We can better able to connect with our feelings and surrender and release them because of the joy we experience with dance. It's a great daily stress releaser. Couple's dance in particular is wonderful because of the touch and the harmonizing of beat and rhythms. It interweaves energies and therefore raises consciousnesses together. It's truly wonderful to see a couple dancing together in harmony. They are dancing as one. It's true love!

Bioenergetic Exercises

The bioenergetic exercises are awesome in helping one to dislodge suppressed and repressed feelings. Through bioenergetic exercises we enable ourselves to create the emotional space to better access and address our issues. The exercises have enabled us to create a physiological process that expedites surrender and release of feelings through connected circular breathing. An example of a bioenergetic exercise would include standing, arms extended (or fists placed in the lower back), inhale as you bend your knees and exhale as you rise to a standing position.

Play

I love to watch children play. They chase each other, communicate in an animated way, create informal relationships, resolve conflicts, create relationships, have fun, create community, learn acrobatics, learn from each other, and learn to explore new environments. Play is essential in helping one to help oneself evolve mentally, emotionally, creatively, intuitively, physically, and most importantly, joyfully.

The Buddhist Hug

I enjoy sharing a "Buddhist hug" with some individuals. The Buddhist hug uses a focused breath and is done three times with the use of the "integrated, silent, divine, circular, connected, transformational breath method." The individuals synchronize their breath together. They begin by pulling in oxygen as they embrace. The stomach inflates and then there is a slow exhale in unison. The first two hugs are a giving and receiving to each other and the third hug is done in harmony and connection with the divine spirit! Most people respond or react by saying its divinely relaxing and empowering.

Points to Ponder:

Can bioenergetic exercises, dance, and other forms of motion aid you in your self-development?

Are there other types of movements that better resonate with you?

Do you play with your friends, children, significant others?

Have you ever realized the significance of play in your self-development?

Do you realize how physical movement is necessary for your health and well-being on a daily basis?

How does it feel to embrace another human being? Would you consider attempting a "Buddhist hug"?

CHAPTER 16

Our Creative Nuances

Imagination is better than knowledge.
—Albert Einstein

The chakra of the thyroid/throat. The enhancement of the mental and emotional body impacts directly the expansion and evolvement of the intuitive person. It's here where we trigger our ability to *imagine*! It's our imagination and our wonder that is a dynamic quality that all humankind experiences. It's from here where we can visualize the wonders of the multicolored rainbow. It's here where we can take journeys to faraway places and experience how life would be in other provinces, states, countries, planets, and universes. It's here where we journey into inner alternate states of consciousness. We dream and envision our dreams coming true. We create reality different from our past and present. Our wonder, our imagination, our dreams are the prerequisites for the use of our creativity that can function as a bridge in our healing, personal growth, expansion, evolution, revolution of ourselves, and growing in our spiritual power.

Magic is yet another manifestation of our creative mind. We have the ability to perform magic, to create wonder and mystery for ourselves and others. Your responsible sexual reproduction is yet another quality of creation. It's perhaps the most magnificent of our creative biological talents. It's also fun!

Humankind's folklore is based on verbal stories handed down from one generation to the next. Someone in the chain makes a decision to write down the stories. The stories are documented in the form of myths, fables, legends, parables, and fairy tales.

Myths are unusual legendary narratives that present parts of the beliefs of a people or explain a practice or natural phenomenon. It is an imaginary or unverifiable person or thing. Enchantment is another component of our creative powers. "Alice in Wonderland" and "The Wizard of Oz" are examples of enchanting children's stories.

I recently participated as an audience member watching "Imagination Express All-Aboard!" This is a group of mime performers raising students' consciousness through their performances by way of mime. I watched the mime performers as they focused on creating the consciousness that awakens our ability to make choices. They were able to communicate through their mime performance the choice of free will. We can choose to personalize in a hurtful way others' thoughtless comments or choose to intelligently find another solution. I describe more about "Imagination Express All-Aboard" below.

IMAGINATION EXPRESS ALL-ABOARD

Rosemarie Ballard describes
"Imagination Express All Aboard" as follows:

The intention of this company is to educate children on the importance of body movement and self expression. The goal is to affect as many children as possible. The company has been together since 1996 and has worked at several children's and arts festival all over Southern California. They are presently giving performances and workshops through the San Diego school system. The members of the company are dedicated to keeping mime a recognized art form. The players also enjoy entertaining the big kids at parties, corporate events, and street fairs. The spontaneous standing ovation given by 220 children at a recent workshop lets the company know that they are on the right track.

Here are some excerpts from some of the skits that "Imagination Express—All Aboard" perform. These skits are motivational in form, creative; promote transcendence and transformation of human behaviors.

• You Can Do It If You Try!

In this poignant autobiographical piece, Rosemarie Ballard, one of the performers, chronicles her addiction to cigarettes. Her smoking habit then turns into a fetish for food. She gains a great deal of weight and exercises it off until she is restored to her old svelte and healthy self. Rosemarie uses this piece as a platform to discourage kids from smoking and to encourage smokers to quit.

• The Park

We have a scene at a bench in the park in which a little girl with bubble gum gets herself into a sticky situation. A balloon salesman literally gets carried away with his wares, helping a pigeon with a broken wing to fly. We break the fourth wall, inviting the audience to share in our illusions with a sly hobo who panhandles to the crowd and a boy who plays catch with an invisible ball. A pair of cantankerous senior citizens shares a bench and learns that the world doesn't have to be so lonely when you have each other.

- ## Turn of the Crank

The cycle of addiction turns ugly as our protagonist becomes addicted to methamphetamine. His highs get shorter, and his downs worsen as he gives up everything to satisfy his habit. Finally, he breaks the cycle and climbs the mountain of recovery.

- ## Willpower

It is here where we have an emotional food fight and a struggle with the refrigerator over healthy eating habits.

- ## Timber

A lumberjack tests his mettle against a gigantic tree. The relentless lumberjack upgrades his arsenal of tools, pulling each one from a magic carpet bag. The tree stands, unmoved by his efforts, but ultimately, the lumberjack's persistence and resourcefulness pays off.

What's Your Sign?
(Harassment and Self-Esteem)

Two bullies in white masks harass a girl who has difficulty reading. They taunt her with "stupid" signs until she accepts the moniker and hangs it around her neck. She is miserable until someone changes her sign from "stupid" to "wonderful." Accepting this new moniker, she stands straighter, finding new confidence in herself. We challenge the audience to think about what they believe about themselves and what they say to others. "We could relate to the one where they were making fun of the girl. I think that everyone has been in that position once in their lifetime."

Student, Mar Vista High School

I used mime in the classroom successfully to teach English as a Second Language to Special Education and Second Language learners five to six years of age. The small children were completely fascinated by the use of movement, fantasy, imagination, and reality. They all had speech and limited attention disabilities. They functioned to a very significant degree on an intuitive level. Their learning ability was quite intuitive. The mime was in particular significant in helping them learn. Mime teaches on a very intuitive level.

Savannah Ray was one of my special education students who has a speech impediment. Savannah was of Asian heritage and very sweet and sensitive. She was a particularly intelligent little girl who was able to learn extremely well because of mime.

Consciousness Quotient

It's important for us to train ourselves to stay conscious about our thoughts and our feelings in order to expand and evolve. We can begin an inner quest when we are conscious of our underlying feelings. A red flag goes up when a thought and feeling is present that doesn't serve us. It is then time to address the negative self-defeating thought. We can contradict the negative thought with a positive one. We create tension in doing so! We can once again release our emotional tension by manifesting the feelings in a physiological way.

It's in being proactive where our evolution and expansion can occur! It's in our being proactive and doing the inner exploration where our emotional adventure begins. We begin to explore the emotions and experience the feelings in our emotional body as we progress. Our exploration into the unknown begins and our journey unfolds. We can choose to use our creativity in our exploration to explore different feelings. It's truly a journey of discovery! We can create tension from our memories. We can then begin to physiological and emotionally process our feelings.

Creating the Consciousness Through the Use of Parables of Ancient Wisdom

Dr. Julia Taylor holds a class on parables at her house. She feels "parables" are a catalyst for raising awareness, helping people help themselves become more conscious of their behaviors and more conscious of their relationship with and to others. Dr. Julia speaks with a wonderful southern dialect and comes from the state of Arkansas.

Confidentiality

We can use a parable to interpret circumstances and situations that unfold in our own lives.
"Sharp Sword" is Dr. Julia Taylor's favorite.
The two warriors meet. One says to the other, "I've got a sharp sword." The other warrior says, "Prove it." So the warrior cuts his head off." So the head is rolling down the hill and the head says, "YES! THAT REALLY WAS A SHARP SWORD!" What can we learn from this parable?

Dr. Julia explained. That guy didn't have the big picture in mind. The other way to look at it is this: He got his head chopped off to learn how to tap into other ways of coping in the world. The moral of the parable is we cannot think in narrow terms but maintain a flexible viewpoint. When we think in narrow terms we limit the range of our choices.
A narrow point of view does not serve our higher self nor does it serve the well-being of others. It may in fact be hurtful to self and others. It's a learning experience for our personal growth and spiritual enlightenment.

Parables Are Inspirational as Well

Parables are consciousness rising. They increase awareness. "It's looking for other meaning where things may have been bad," claims Dr. Taylor. We learn to take another point of view and learn from our experiences. It's important to change one's reaction and think about a variety of responses. It's important to engage in discussion about parables in a group. It's a way of rising consciousness so we move into compassion, grace, love, knowledge and go beyond our emotional reactions to a greater truth.

The Horse Race

Shakespeare states, "What's in a name? A rose
by any other name would smell as sweet."

There were approximately nine horses in the race at the Del Mar Race Track, Del Mar, California. D and DFL bumped each other in the stretch. D placed first and was the winner, and DFL placed second at the finish. There was joy and cheers by the bettors who held the winning ticket!

D and DFL bumped each other in the stretch. There was a protest! There was a sigh by those who held the winning ticket, and those who held second place held their breath awaiting the final decision. The jockeys who were designated judges viewed the video of the two horses bumping each other in the stretch while the race track bettors sitting among the crowd held their tickets in hand. They patiently awaited the final declaration of winner in the race!
The word came from the judges, the decision was made, the judges decided to reverse their decision. There was a groan that emerged from the holders of the ticket with the letter D! Now it was DFL the winner, and it was D who placed second in the race! The parable is D who placed first initially and was disqualified and placed second, his name was Denied and DFL who initially placed second and was now designated the winner because of the judges viewing the video, his name was Designed for Luck.

Parable of Loss

I came to know Rachel over the years after meeting her many times at a spiritual book discussion group. She came to the group one evening and exclaimed that "I just came from the doctor who claimed I've been afflicted with breast cancer." She claimed she was angry because the doctor had given her two weeks to live. Perhaps she needed to accept the doctor's diagnosis.

Rachel, had a lovable and feisty personality. She would come to the group wearing and dressed many times as a clown. She believed in making people happy. She was a so-called funologist. She organized workshops around the theme of fun. She focused on helping people to laugh at themselves as she laughed at the pain in her life in a fun and creative way. She thought that if a person can transcend her pain then she inevitably transforms and is free. She would exclaim, "Fun works!" I guess spirit needed her to organize her workshops in another dimension. Rachel claimed she would seek out the opinion of another physician regarding her illness. Rachel made her transition one month later.

I went to a Sunday morning metaphysical church service and met Jackie a member of my yoga group and told her the story of Rachel. I would be attending her memorial the very next day at the women's club. I told her of Rachel's diagnosis of breast cancer. Jackie was a retired psychologist and was a gentle, loving, good-natured soul. Jackie then confided in me that in fact she was also diagnosed with breast cancer and that the physicians were watching her closely for any severe changes in her condition. I focused my attention deliberately to listen to Jackie as tears began to well up in her eyes. I felt shocked at her revelation. Sometimes I feel angry at spirit because he chooses to take kind, loving, good-natured people from me. I'm selfish and just want them to stay. Their leaving just reinforces a sad sense of loneliness, a sense of loss within me. I choose to release my sadness and permit and allow these warm, good-natured spirits to transition. It's in the nature and evolution of life and death.

I used the integrated, circular, divine, transformational breath to connect, surrender, and release my sadness. I manifested and released my feelings of sadness by animated laughter and tears. It's truly a *joy* to have the ability to feel my feelings whatever they may be and not to ignore or be in denial of them. I feel a sense of relief because of the emotional release.

Frog Cookie Jar and Snake

I met Karen Kozlow at devotional singing many years ago. Karen is a seasoned veteran of the arts and craft movement. She lights up the room with her bubbling, effervescent smile and personality. She discovered her niche in her life by designing ceramics professionally. She brings a strong spiritual quality to her ceramic pieces.

Kozlow has created whimsical pieces in clay since 1976 which are fully functional. Her bright, colorful creations are used as vases, dinnerware, cookie jars, bells, soup tureens, teapots, and much more. Most of her work is influenced by Matisse. She has a line of beautiful Matisse dinnerware, three-dimensional miniatures, and wall and floor pieces. Her whimsical "Frog Cookie Jug" is especially colorful. I love its big blue poke-dot head, black-and-white pupil eyes, and red kissable lips, yellow outstanding ladle for a tongue, bulging yellow stomach, and long white-colored wraparound hands. One cannot help but want to give this frog a warm lovable embrace!

Karen lost her home and all her paintings in the disastrous 1969 Pine Valley fire in California, but her ceramics and fighting spirit pulled through. When Kozlow discovered her ceramics had survived she cemented them together, grew plants in them—a sort of growing-out-of the-ashes kind of thing—and put on an art show called "Disaster Works."

She enjoys a work space at her home in Leucadia, California, which consists of a studio with many windows. The natural light shining through the windows is inspirational in her view and enhances her creative talents

She comes from a fine arts background in painting. She has shown at craft fairs, contemporary crafts markets, and Buyers Market of American Crafts among others. She has done a variety of craft shows at locations as Tiffany's windows of Beverly Hills, the La Jolla Museum of Contemporary Art, UCSD and San Diego State University. She is listed in *Who's Who in American Crafts.*

Points to Ponder:

What is your consciousness quotient?

How creative and vivid is your imagination?

Have you experienced the intellectual consciousness-raising experiences of the aspects of folklore, mime, and crafts?

What parables are there in your life?

What creative inclinations do you have?

CHAPTER 17

Need to Be in Community:
Our Social Body

Community support is a quality necessary for our surrender and release of energies that do not serve us. It's said to be the chakra where we experience our empathy and compassion. It is necessary to bond in and with community members. We create a catalyst and pathway to spiritual connection within by bonding with each other. It's the divine spark and its spiritual connection to community that supports our universal connection. The support enables us to feel secure enough to explore our inner frontiers and go where we have not gone before. Community bonding creates a catalyst and pathway to nourish ourselves holistically.

Belonging

In Maslow's "Higher Order of Needs" the need to belong is essential (*Motivation and Personality*, 1954). Mutual giving and receiving are the essence of strong relationships. Cooperation opens the heart, mind, and soul to divine energy for all. Community is the need to share with each other. Bonding is woven and created within through music. The song by Malaya reflects that opening to spirit and the love that flows through self and community.

Each and Every Moment

Each and every moment
I'm opening to you

Each and every moment
I'm opening to you
Your love is flowing through

Each and every moment
I'm opening to you
Your love is flowing through

Each and every moment
Your love is flowing through

Oh, your love is flowing through!
Oh, your love is flowing through!
Oh, your love is flowing through!

Love is flowing through!
Love is flowing through!

The love of spirit flows through community! Spiritual community
begins through effective, focused, and efficient listening to thoughts,
feelings, and an awareness of body language! It's about intelligent
caring, empathy, and compassion!

We hopefully come to experience friendship, joy, play, and love
with our primary family and through our affiliation with secular
spiritual groups. We have the potential of experiencing both
enlightenment and divine personal power in our spiritual
connections with others. The interaction of listening skills joined
with our spiritual activities (dances of universal peace, tantra, yoga,
church groups) manifests our spiritual power.

I've been a member of the international peer counseling community since 1972 and have met many wonderful cocounselors throughout the world. I've participated at many workshops with cocounselors and have experienced many fine relationships. Through this community I've been able to focus effectively, efficiently, and persistently. I've shed both emotional and physical wounds and expanded and evolved joyfully! What a spiritual, empowering experience!

I belong to another secular spiritual community in San Diego, California, where I participate in spiritual prayer, folk dance, group singing, meditation, pot lucks, concerts, nature retreats, and nonnative American sweat lodges. I've also known friendship and acceptance because of these diverse groups of people.

We often ask ourselves what the determining emotional factor of community is. When two people are there for each other in an empathetic manner is certainly one criteria of community. We learn to feel safe enough to express vulnerability and insecurity in a spiritual connection. We learn to receive and give loving attention when we listen and express our vulnerability and insecurities to each other. We learn cooperation with each other in service to each other.

The Brainstorming or Group's "New Group Thought"

Group consensus and brainstorming is fundamentally a community and social interaction.
What is true for the individual is dynamically true for the group. It's a reason for the importance of meetings. In the brainstorming there is an attempt at conscious, clear, and concise formulation of thoughts, feelings, ideas, conclusions, actions, and to follow through and follow up. Brainstorming takes place in any group, organization, city, state, country, or world.

Foster Lodge

The Sierra Club had invited me to do one transformational breath class at their retreat in the beautiful Laguna Mountains, six thousand feet above sea level overlooking the vast timelessness of the San Diego County Anza Borrego Desert below. The Sierra Club is dedicated to preserving the back country wilderness. They are committed to sharing nature in a rational way with the world.

The Laguna Mountains are majestic, mysterious, and overpowering in their ability to capture and hold the endless heavens above and the sky's beige and green colors. One of the members of the Sierra Club had heard me interviewed over the radio and had invited me to participate as a workshop facilitator.

The road to Foster Lodge was a tributary from the Sunrise Highway. The lodge is hidden from the outside world. There were approximately fifty people attending the weekend holistic retreat.

The people had come to experience a wide variety of holistic workshops. There was a willingness on the part of this community to do emotional work. I'm inspired to lead groups when people are willing to do the inner work to transform their self-defeating behaviors; to expand themselves intellectually, emotional, and spiritually, to improve their personal relationships; and to create more peace, bliss, kindness, and satisfaction for themselves and others.

I was scheduled to do but one workshop. The first one was quite successful, and the group became inspired. The people asked for an additional session. Once again the participants were motivated by my working with them and requested yet a third transformational experience. The members claimed that the process had helped them address their emotional and physical wounds and enabled them to feel better. It was the first experience for many participants, and they were energized by the circular breath technique. The third meeting was attended by seventeen individuals and once again it was successful. The group experience in a community setting helped support people and encouraged them to help themselves in a healthy nonthreatening way.

I followed up with the participants who claimed the work helped them to confront and surrender feelings from within their emotional body. They were inspired!

Whole Living Retreat

It was the Fourth of July weekend and, we came together in community at Palomar Mountain in Southern California for a "Whole Living Retreat"!

We gathered in a group and drove to the top of Palomar Mountain and hiked through the woods. We were approximately fifteen people. The leader shared with us a location on the path where Native American Indians gathered in community. This was a location where centuries before Native American Indians used rocks to mash acorns for food. There were-well shaped holes in solid granite where the Native Americans labored to produce the edible grains.

We spied a beautiful deer behind some trees that was observing our every movement. The doe seemed so fragile with its thin legs, olive brown body, white bushy tail, and elongated ears. The elongated ears were so necessary for the warning sounds of mountain lions who roamed the forest and pastures of the Cleveland National Park. I loved watching its movements through the wooded area. She never took her eyes off of our group as it managed its ballet-type steps through the heavy wooded brush.

There was an abundance of musicians for the celebration. Among them there was Elivia Melody and her crystal bowls. The bowls were of different sizes, and their vibrations are said to have healing, expanding, evolving sounds, which are catalysts to the healing and expansion of the self. The tones of the crystal bowls are conducive to elevating spirit within and provide a catalyst as a connection with our spirit and the divine spirit. Elivia and her assistant play the multiple-sized crystals bowls and the sounds that emanate from their celestial shapes created greater peace and tranquility for the meditative audience who were present.

The musicians included Bill who played the didgeridoo, a long-shaped pipe, and Joan who played the oud, the zephyr, and the flute. The instruments and skill of the musicians only added to the loving tones that helped all to feel at peace.

Adult Day Care

I was employed as a teacher at an adult day health care center. The adults share companionship and enjoy group activities together. The illnesses and idiosyncrasies abound! It's almost a model for a class in psychology. The adults have a myriad of illnesses including paranoia, schizophrenia, down syndrome depression, and other mental and emotional diseases.

The adult day health care residents are so vulnerable, sensitive, sweet, and intelligent. One cannot help but to love them.

Elizabeth had a habit of picking up things that were dropped. She did that consistently. She had such a warm and sensitive heart. Her facial expression seldom changed. It seemed part of her was just not there! She was Filipino. She was a woman who stood approximately 5'4" tall, stocky built, with black hair, and brown eyes. She spoke slowly but very distinctly. I did a lesson where I deleted the vowels from the words and she responded very favorably to announcing the vowels that were missing. I found it interesting that she was so responsive to the vowels.

The world of the adult day health care is surreal. The residents experience a great deal of depression. The situation is emotional and physically trying for the adults. I enjoyed being creative and helping the members of my class enjoy their experience. They just had a need to focus their attention on the positive and not on their difficulties. They needed to focus their attention on the geography and English in order to enrich their reality.

Today we had a celebrity party. The members of my class pretended to be actors, actresses, and singers. They really had fun becoming the characters! I asked them to think of individuals who they would really like to portray.

The class members choose celebrities such as Frank Sinatra, Dick Van Dyke, Sylvester Stallone, Jackie Onassis, Batman, Marilyn Monroe, John Wayne, and Tom Hanks. They certainly had fun with their choices.

Points to Ponder:

Do you participate in any social or community events?
Are you a member of a spiritual or political club or sporting community?
Do you have an interest in a personal growth or book discussion group?
Are you active in any service group with children or disabled seniors?

CHAPTER 18

The Nuances of the Heart Body

Spirit of the Living God, descend upon my heart.
Dwell within and let thy love flow to light the world.

—Val Cooper
Midtown Church
of Religious Science

It is in the heart chakra where we experience the quality of "love"—the powerful healing quality of all our dips, bumps, potholes, and craters we encounter in our lives. People feel like they are having a heart attack because of stress. I have often felt stress building around the heart muscle or as I like to say the heart chakra. It amazes me the profound sense of relaxation felt following a release of stress surrounding this energy meridian. I experience this by practicing conscious healing breath or a peer counseling session. It's truly a miracle!

Emotional Giving and Receiving

This reflects the heart chakra. Giving and receiving is a significant component in personal growth. We learn to take responsibility for being there for another human being. Sharing a material possession or human quality is a way of building human character. We enhance the spirit! When we state heartfelt words of appreciation we give from a human point of view. It has the impact of opening the heart chakra and a door to spirituality. We acknowledge other human beings which reflects our self-worth. When we give in a heartfelt way, the action increases our self-esteem. The emotional giving opens the door to expanding both human trust and hope. Our act creates authentic hope and trust. The giving and receiving becomes spiritual power. It's a healthy action to take!

Stress and Depression Cause Heart Disease

Stress and depression definitively aggravate heart disease. We can learn to surrender and release stress and distress around the heart chakra in many ways. One way is through the words of this beautiful melody that I learned at devotional singing.

Deep in My Heart

Deep in my heart, o Great Spirit
Deep in my heart, o Great Spirit

Deep in my heart is a song of prayer
O Great Spirit, you are always there.

I am light, I am ever free
I am life throughout eternity
To this world we have chosen to come
We are ever one, ever one, and ever one.

© 2003 by Inner Harmony Music
Words and music by Michael Stillwater.

Beth Ivy
"Remembrance"

I was a friend of Beth Ivy who made her transition recently. She was a young wonderful musician and passionate soul with a giving heart! The poem below is in remembrance of her loving heart and spirit!

LOOK FOR ME NOT WITH SORROW IN THE
PLACE WHERE I ONCE WAS, FOR
I AM NO LONGER THERE.

INSTEAD, REJOICE FOR ME AS I STEP EVER
SO LIGHTLY ASCENDING THE STAIRWAY TO
HEAVEN'S GATE, NOW JOYFULLY JOINED IN
HERALDING MY ARRIVAL AND MY
REUNION WITH THE ONE.

WE SING IN CELESTIAL CONCERT
THROUGHOUT ETERNITY, AND I FEEL
A NEWFOUND FREEDOM, HERETOFORE
UNEXPLORED, UNEXPERIENCED,
UNEXPRESSED.

WEEP NOT FOR ME, ONLY SEEK MY
PASSIONATE PRESENCE IN THE INNOCENT
EYES OF CHILDREN, THE HEALING COMFORT
OF ANIMALS, THE RADIANCE OF THE SUN AT
DAWN AND THE SHOOTING STARS I RIDE TO
ECHO MY SOULFUL SONG OF HOPE FOR
HUMANITY THROUGHOUT THE GALAXY.
I AM ALWAYS WITH YOU.

By Sacha Rana of
"The Messages"

Sacha Rana was a beloved friend of Beth Ivy. She tells a story
about her spiritual connection to Beth Ivy following Beth's
transition into a new dimension.

Sacha had gone on three different occasions to a local store that
fosters spiritual awareness in the sales of its wares. They play
spiritual music in the store. It was on three different, "random"
occasions shortly following Beth Ivy's transition that Sacha claims

to have heard the same melody. Sacha experienced these occurrences as synchronistic and as a spiritual message emanating from her beloved friend. Sacha interpreted these messages from Beth Ivy that all was well and that Beth Ivy's love of and for Sacha was ever present!

Transition of Spiritual Leader Robert Fry

The much-loved spiritual leader and musician Robert Fry made his transition in the state of Hawaii in June 2004 at a young age. He will be missed by many because of his heartfelt and selfless giving of his love. He gave his love through his music and his leadership qualities in spiritual community. Many experienced his human qualities as a blessing because of his ability to facilitate dances of universal peace, tantra, devotional singing, healing breathwork, and participation in courses on miracles. Some of his songs such as "I Am Opening to Love," "Love Is the Feeling I'm Living in My Heart," and "I Am Opening" appear in the first book *I Dare to Heal with Compassionate Love*. In honor of his passing I include the sacred Sufi prayer and invocation of Hazrat Inayat Khan:

O Thou, who are the perfection of love, harmony and beauty, Lord of heaven and Earth, open my heart that I may hear your voice, which constantly comes from within. Disclose to me your Divine Light which is hidden in my Soul, that I may know and understand life better. Most merciful and compassionate God, give me your great goodness, teach me your loving forgiveness, raise me above the distinctions and differences which separate me, send me the peace of your Divine Spirit, and unite me with your Perfect Being.

Amen.

Points to Ponder:

Have you ever had the experience of giving of yourself in a heartfelt way?

Do you know any heartfelt music that you can share with others?

Have you ever experienced synchronistic circumstances?

Are you aware of the fact that heart disease can have a relationship to severe stressful or distressful circumstances?

Do you love yourself in a heartfelt way? If so, how do you actively do it!

CHAPTER 19

Steps to Our Spiritual Power and Enlightenment

Devotional Singing
Oh Mother Earth
Your heart beats in me.
Oh Father Sky
Your breath I breathe.
Oh little children
Your hands I hold.
Oh sister and brother together
Together we grow.

There is also "omniscient" learning, a learning that opens to infinite alertness to and awareness of, understanding, and insight! I believe the nuances of "omniscient learning" are those which enable us to experience our eternal soul. I believe that developing conscious, infinite awareness is synchronistic to our soul development. They comprise the following:

Alertness

We can become a healthy human being by becoming alert to those circumstances and situations that trigger those thoughts that restimulate our past hurts and distresses. We can become aware of our healthy and unhealthy behaviors by way of how others act and react to us or by becoming alert to our feelings in our own worlds.

We can become alert to addressing those fears, angers, and sadness by implementing tools we have developed to release unnecessary feelings. We can become alert to our thoughts that will trigger those feelings. The thought "We're in charge now or we're taking charge of the world right now [meaning our own world]" can be used.

We can become a *conscious* human being by becoming alert to our healthy and unhealthy behaviors. Being conscious of our environment and its impact on us is essential. We often are unaware of the environment and its impact upon us.

We can learn to become alert to our body armor. Our body armor prevents us from addressing our feelings. They are our inhibitions. We can react because of our inhibitions or we can consciously decide to become alert to our inhibitions and unhealthy behaviors. We can counter our reaction by responding with positive thoughts, feelings and then a positive attitude.

Awareness

What is our cognitive and emotional frequency of our awareness to our environment? What is our cognitive and emotional awareness to our suppressed and repressed feelings that mirror our thoughts? How aware are we to the thoughts that run through our mind and how those thoughts can trigger feelings of anger, fear, and sadness? How aware are we of our environment and how does the environment trigger thoughts of emotion? How aware are we of our sensations? Are those sensations an ongoing emotional disturbance? The sensations linger. Do we feel the sensations in an ongoing way? How aware are we of our past hurts and traumas and how our present circumstances and situations can trigger those thoughts that can trigger feelings of anger, fear, and sadness in all of their depths, degrees, and emotional dimensions of emotional time and space? How aware are we of our unhealthy behaviors in the world? How aware are we of our healthy behaviors in the world?

We can decide and choose to become conscious of those behaviors and the reactions and feelings that correspond to them or we can decide and choose to be unaware of them and ignore them. We usually ignore others' reactions and responses to us unless we are sensitive and conscious of their thoughts and behaviors in relationship to ourselves.

Intention

Intention can motivate us to action. We intend to build a house. We intend to create a beautiful picture. We intend to meet a woman. The intention puts in motion, a thought, and a feeling. The result is the action.

When thought and feeling are connected with each other there is clear resonance of intention. When thought and feeling are disconnected with each other there is clear dissonance in intention. We may very well succeed despite dissonance only because of our willingness to do so! When we take action then thought and feeling begin their congruency, connection, and completion.

It's important to be clear about our intention. Clarity is essential. Doubt and reservation can get in the way. The use of our resources, our tools to remove the negative feelings that surface are essential. We may need to remove fear, anger, and sadness. The meditation and counseling techniques help us to remove the dissonant emotions that surface. Intention is clear when we are alert and aware of our dissonant emotions.

Learning Courage

Our courage comes from our heart body. We need an emotionally empowered heart muscle. "Cour" comes from the French language. We need the "cour" to consistently address our emotional body that stores the feelings reflective of our issues. We can find the courage to look at our difficulties by making a consistent decision to address them.

Learning Faith and the Faith Comes

Our disposition, our sensitivities, our temperament, our personalities, our genetic, biological, developmental makeup are being stressed by the environmental demands of our society. This has negative and positive impact on our mental, emotional, and spiritual bodies. What choices do we have to meet these demands?

I have chosen faith! We choose faith because of life's circumstances, because of the physical and emotional dips, bumps, potholes, and craters in our lives, because we have situations that are beyond our control. When we are alert and aware of our thoughts we decrease our vulnerability to the world. We are vulnerable because of our past wounds. We must stay positive and have faithful thoughts.

We must stay aware when fearful thoughts arise within us! It is here where we intrude or interrupt upon those fearful thoughts and replace them with faithful thoughts which cause us to be positive regardless of our circumstances, situations, wounds, dips, bumps, potholes, and craters. We use our tools and methods that we have developed to release any tensions and help ourselves to achieve faithful thoughts and therefore achieve our goals and purpose.

When life doesn't seem to go our way we can choose to feel our feelings and then always focus on what we have. We can literally list exactly what we have and think and be grateful for that which is in and who is in our lives. When we act in this way we have the potential of expanding and growing. When we focus on what we have and the good in our lives it impacts our attitude with ourselves and with others.

Tenacity

Tenacity comes from our "will." We strengthen our will through our positive thoughts, through our positive attitude, but more importantly through our negotiating our feelings that *need* to be negotiated effectively, efficiently, consistently, and with focus. We derive the maximum benefit of negotiating our feelings by acting in a way that is healthy for ourselves and others. This can necessitate acting selflessly for others if and when necessary. We believe our children and parents must be respected and, if need be, come first before ourselves. If and when we have a conflict of whose needs come first we can always invoke personal spiritual power. We seek a solution and make a decision by moving to a higher state of consciousness.

Self-Discipline

The word "disciple" is included in the word "discipline." I define the word "disciple" as a convinced adherent to a discipline. It's important to become a disciple of a discipline or disciplines to maintain faith in self, others, and a universal entity. We can always use a method/tool that resonates with us to maintain our focus, center ourselves, and resolve suppressed and repressed feelings that have been triggered by situations and circumstances. This will help us to continue to expand and evolve our personal growth. I recommend a martial art to learn self-discipline. This may include a form of chi-gong, tai chi chih, taekwondo, karate, aikido, or whatever method that resonates with you. The key is to maintain a discipline that moves out that energy in the body that doesn't serve you. The other key is to be consistent in its practice. It's essential that the practice resolves feelings.

Maintaining a consciousness of and a stable connection to awareness, alertness, intention, courage, faith, tenacity, and self-discipline are just not enough. We must also maintain an intention to maintain a consciousness of surrender, release, and liberation from our embodied dark and shadow emotion. We will then find ourselves in a secure harbor with our spiritual power.

Acknowledging/Recognizing the Significance of the Components of the Self

I usually state that emotion reflects the ocean, the soul reflects the desert, and the spirit reflects the mountains. Here I speak about the many facets of the self in the pyramid and how each facet has its unique qualities, needs, wants, and desires. Each body component needs, yearns, wants, wills, and calls to be nurtured in its own unique way. We must be open to its calling and be aware, alert, and considerate of its unique needs, desires, and yearnings. We gradually learn to do all the above naturally and with grace. We can then be assured to relax.

Sincerity of Purpose

Are we sincere in our purpose in addressing those issues that we need to acknowledge and recognize? Our sincerity of purpose is usually hindered by our fears. Defense mechanisms and defenses get in our way of feeling our fears. We need to learn to address our denial, negative aspects of ego and beliefs, and beliefs systems that get in our way of our intentions and of our purpose. How sincere are we of our purpose?

Address

We address our negative and/or unhealthy thoughts by changing them and hopefully transforming our feelings. There are many times that attempting to cognitively transform our thoughts are just not good enough to transform our feelings. We must find effective methods and tools that directly address our feelings to bring about a transformation of our attitude.

Access

We learn to access the feelings in our emotional body. We can use the connected healing breath as a tool to accomplish this goal. The power of the breath takes charge of the emotional depth, degree, and dimension of feelings we choose to access. We choose and regulate our breath by deciding how deep a breath we choose to take and therefore the power of release that occurs! We are in charge!

Connection

We connect with the unhealthy emotions. We begin to touch the suppressed (in the collective consciousness) and repressed feelings (in the collective unconsciousness). We begin to touch upon and connect with sadness, anger, fear in their depths, degrees, and their emotional time and space dimensions. When we connect with the depth and degree of emotion we also begin to connect with the density and intensity of feelings. We touch upon and begin to connect by way of the breath. The more profound the breath, the greater density and intensity of the emotion we connect with. We do this by permitting and allowing ourselves to use the stomach muscles to pull oxygen into the root or pelvic chakra. Our stomach inflates with oxygen. We feel the feelings building in our stomach. We feel the body-mind connection taking place. It is when we feel this connection when we surrender and release our feelings reflective of that emotion we are harboring in our body. Here we are in charge of the depth, degree, and dimension of our breathing. We take responsibility, and we decide!

I also touch upon and begin to connect with my shadow and dark feelings by way of meditation, listening to classical music, or by other means which resonate with me!

Dimensions

Physics claims a multitude of dimensions. This is also true of emotion! There are the emotional dimensions of time and space—up and down, back and forth, left and right, and a series of other emotional dimensions that are in a haze of shadow and darkness. They are within the emotional body because we can feel it. We know intuitively that the emotions are within our inner frontiers. We become aware of the emotional dimensions of our wounds when we begin to focus effectively and efficiently.

The Body in Knowing, the Body Consciousness, the Body Knows

We need to develop an ability to listen to the body messages and the body calling to us. We cannot ignore its callings, messages, yearnings, and its needs. We must develop an awareness of our body talking to us. It will call to us! We need to be sensitive and listen to our body's groans, syllables, sounds, energies, and its desires. The body physiologically always knows when and what it will and can connect to. We are prepared to connect to the shadow and dark dimensions reflective of our awareness. It becomes our choice to tread on the doorstep and knock on the innermost crevices of our emotional body and connect with our inner sanctum.

Support

We reach out for support from others (if necessary) to help us help ourselves achieve our transformation. We may need to be nurtured by others. We do this, for example, by participation in groups. There are groups such as (CODA) Codependence Anonymous, martial art forms, spiritual counseling, peer counseling, song and dance gatherings. We use our groups for nurturing of ourselves and others.

Self-Support

We can learn to counsel ourselves through the foregoing concepts. After we have adequately practiced with another cocounselor we develop an inner peer counselor whom we can go to and support our process effectively. This is a wonderful intuitive skill.

Points to Ponder:

Are you willing to learn and practice the steps to your personal spiritual power and enlightenment?

Would you consider your own awareness, alertness, and intention as traits that enhance courage, faith, tenacity, self-discipline, sincerity of purpose; traits that address, access, and support yourself in relationship to your own self-realization and liberation?

CHAPTER 20

Cause and Effect

Of the
Genetic, Developmental, Biological, and
Environmental Dynamics of Behavior

The controversy and discussion in psychology is always "Is it nature or nurture that creates the idiosyncratic, healthy or unhealthy behaviors? The answer is yes it is both in the nature and the nurture of humankind where the cause can be found that creates both healthy and unhealthy behaviors. It's the genetic, biological, developmental, and environmental dynamics that are the causes and determines our behaviors. This, in essence, is the basis for all cause-and-effect behaviors.

We can make choices that create joy or create pain in our life. We have the power to decide what is in our interest. We have the power to decide what choices nurture our nature and what choices detract from our nature. If and when we make choices that nurture our nature, we can experience joy, happiness, and a sense of spirituality. If and when we make choices that detract from our nature, we can experience discomfort and pain. There are times we just don't know. We just don't have the adequate information, knowledge, and education. There are times when we are confused because of hurtful patterns that impact our cognitive abilities. Perhaps it is those confused times where we are just too numb by the hurtful patterns to connect with our feelings. There are times when we are acting out in unaware, unconscious and/or conscious patterns of hurt and trauma. There are times where situations and circumstances are not within our control. We learn hopefully from our experiences. We can only do the best we can do to make life easier for ourselves and others who we impact. We hopefully do not create discomfort and pain in our or others' lives. We can only do what we can do and learn from the lessons of our experiences. If and when we show a willingness to learn from our experiences, we can without doubt or reservation achieve the goal of joy and happiness.

Sandy was a seven-year-old boy who always seemed to walk around with a great deal of anger right under the surface. His teachers requested that Sandy take time-out from the class and spend it at a resource center where he could think about his choices. Sandy was always reluctant to return to his classroom environment where his anger was continually triggered and where he continually experienced reprimands. The counselors and teachers attempted to handle Sandy's anger through behavior modification by giving him choices and providing consequences when his behavior continued to be disruptive. The behavior modification methods were unsuccessful and only magnified Sandy's unwillingness to transform his behavior.

There could have been a multitude of reasons for Sandy's anger. I have experienced many children who carry on similar behaviors. The children clearly have been hurt to affect such behaviors. The trauma and hurt usually come from unhealthy, overwhelming experiences that combined with genetic, biological and developmental factors create the triggering of repressed emotions to surface. The surrender and release of negative emotions when they are sufficiently discharged resolves the profoundest of issues. A specialist knowledgeable of emotional components of surrender and release could be of great assistance to Sandy.

Points to Ponder:

What is your awareness of the genetic, biological, developmental, and environmental impact of your behaviors?

What reasonable objectives and goals can you envision?

What behaviors are beyond your capacity for transition and what must you learn to accept?

CHAPTER 21

Just Surrender, Simple Surrender

Co-Dependent Anonymous

You Can't Heal What You Can't Feel!

Conscious surrender is the pathway to both conscious and unconscious emotional and spiritual faith!

The choice was clear; I took charge of my world, I surrendered my fears.

Become a being that is human by becoming one who cannot help but to be consciously conscious of the collective unconscious.

I surrendered to an inner calling of my soul and could not help but to become an introspective seeker of truth, beauty, and love. It was then I knew freedom of spirit, a sense of joy, but above all, within I found true peace!

I surrendered denial and could not help but to find clarity and wisdom! It is was then that I knew human openness.

I realized that I had no control over the circumstances and situation so I surrendered my self-inflicted fear, anger, and sadness and came to know self-forgiveness.

I am alert to, conscious of, and have decided to surrender "that" conscious/unconscious tension in the present moment, the meaning deeply reaches.

My surrender enabled me to "de-light" in myself.

I surrender those energies from within that do not serve me or the world and allow myself to integrate more into the flow of life.

Surrender

A perspective on this crown chakra is that it's the chakra of surrender and release. We learn the integration of total personality, our spiritual aspects, wisdom, and spiritual will. Through the dynamic processes of surrender we achieve perfection, enlightenment, universal consciousness, and spiritual power.

We cognitively prepare ourselves. We think and make a commitment to follow through using inner contemplation and our perception. We prepare our mind, body, soul, spirit intuitively, creatively, and spiritually for the process. We emotionally prepare our bodies to act. The will of an individual plays an important role. There needs to be a conscious commitment to this process, an emotional posturing in attitude, a positive affirmation of and persistence to the affirmation of "I choose to let go." The decision is made by the individual.

There is heightening tension within. Tension has little choice but to escape. The individual has a choice to surrender the intensity of the emotions or suppress/repress them by a variety of means. An individual must have the preparation to facilitate the surrender and release. Without this element the whole process is useless. Here courage and tenacity is essential. Preparation consists of a variety of door openers.

How do we know of those unproductive energies? What emotions resonate with us and what emotions do not? We learn by doing. We use our tools/methods to explore, uncover, and discover them.

These include Eastern and Western modalities. We use the modality that resonates with ourselves and expedites the "letting go." The thought of surrender must be present throughout the whole process. The mind, body, soul, and heart must be creatively, intuitively, and physically prepared as well. We must allow and permit our body to physically let go. The emotional manifestations of release begin to flow through, and we learn to allow and permit them. The feelings flow through our body in whatever form they may take. We learn to succeed through consistent practice, perseverance, and persistence. The manifestations may take a variety of forms like shaking, storming, scratching, sweating, chattering, tears, primal and primordial sounds or may take other forms. We begin to feel a need for them. We must learn to be instantaneously acute to the physiological needs that surface. If and when we do we must allow and permit them to occur. Sound is a significant element in helping us help ourselves to connect with, go into, and go through our feelings. I wrote about the significance of sound as a catalyst to help us to achieve success. We use essentially whatever methods/tools it takes.

We must be willing to allow the emotional manifestations to continue again and again. We can achieve success through self-counsel. I like playing spiritual music while I'm surrendering emotion and practicing bioenergetic exercises so as to create the emotional space which allow the feelings to emanate and flow. The greatest barrier to surrender is our fear. The fear is usually latent and becomes an unconscious barrier. It is here where our intuitive awareness functions as an essential component in helping us to help ourselves.

Deceiving the Inner Body Armor That Prevents Surrender

Our inner body armor prevents us from surrender. We come alert to our inner defenses. I'm aware of the control mechanisms that prevent me from letting go. I feel the *resistance*. The resistance can consist of those items discussed above that *get in the way* in chapter 6. We need to deceive and circumvent the built-in controls of the defense mechanisms our so-called nature's protection from feeling the pain of our bumps, dips, potholes, and emotional craters. We can learn to do this so we once again come to know our emotional body and its infinite connection to our humanness and our human openness. One example is the socialization process. I usually perform a minor movement of my feet while lying on the bed to facilitate release. The minor movement deceives the controls and facilitates release of feelings. I wiggle my feel and wrists as well to release accumulated tension.

The Significance of Learning to Surrender

Surrender isn't giving up the genuine self. It's giving up and letting go of those parts within the self that doesn't serve the healthy and genuine personality. It's letting go of the shadow and the darkness that inhibits the self. It's letting go of those feelings reflective of hurt and trauma. It's a letting go of the nuances of the range of feelings: sadness through grief, anger through rage, and fear through terror. It's the letting go of the negative aspects of our unhealthy ego (edging God out). It's the letting go of the suppressed and repressed feelings associated with our frozen needs impacted from our conception through the earliest of our formative years. This is the essence of surrender and release.

There is no substitute attribute in acquiring knowledge of surrender. It takes experience and practice. It takes learning it in a consistent, persevering, patient, supportive, attentive effort and effortless practical manner. I don't know any more key component than the component of surrender. The more effortless it is practiced, the greater the depth, degree, trust, and emotional dimension one dares to enter. Our confidence expands!

Surrender is the key element and bridge to help us help ourselves make the connection to the divine spirit within and its connection to the universal divine spirit. Spiritual power embodies us as negativity is released from our lives. It's here where we release feelings associated with any and all emotional hurt and trauma. It is the essence of our authenticity.

Empathy

The significance of this human quality sets the stage for the spiritual enfoldment of compassion:

Compassion (Empathy) to, of, for Yourself

We are not present on this earth to fill the unfulfilled emotional needs of others. We can choose to be there for another human being in a tender, caring way, but it's incumbent upon the individual to respond (not react to) their own needs. It's incumbent on the individual to be alert and aware to filling their own needs. We can do this by empathizing with ourselves. We can do this by learning to love ourselves. If it's painful for us we can invoke a variety of methods to negotiate the feelings that are triggered.

We can also use a variety of methods that involve other human beings to help us help ourselves address the feelings that are triggered. We can then replace our pain with compassion through the help of another human being being there for us.

Spiritual (Empathy) Compassion

The highest form of filling our needs is learning to "let go and let God in." We learn to let go of our painful unfulfilled needs and learn to fill that empty space by accepting spiritual compassion. We can learn to reach out for spiritual compassion through, for example, the transformational, connected, circular, healing, divine breath.

Compassion

Compassion is harbored in our heart chakra. The compassion is the bridge to spiritual connection of one's divine spark and with the universal power of creation itself. Our self-compassion and the compassion we extend to others is the cutting edge that facilitates surrender and that facilitates release. The process becomes our infinite connection with spiritual energy within and in the wide universe.

We bring compassion into those areas of ourselves where our emotional needs require fulfilling. We bring light into our spirit, and in doing so, we illuminate and anchor our spirit to our nature.

We need human connection, tender loving care, for our emotional body. However, it may not be possible for a variety of reasons to receive and get this need filled from another human being. We may not be able to experience an intimacy with another human being. We may not be able to experience warmth and love from another because of hurt and trauma. If and when this is the situation and circumstances then we may need to release the pain of our unfulfilled need. We can then choose to connect with our pain energy, surrender and release it, and be open to receiving divine compassion from spirit.

Respond by Assertion

The energy of compassion opens the floodgate to our asserting ourselves and is the catalyst to release.

Intuitive Surrender

We can use the power of our intuition as a catalyst to help to begin the process of surrender. We know intuitively. Our intuition guides us to the suppressed and repressed feelings.

Thoughtful Surrender

We must think through in a focused and thoughtful way our
goal of surrender. Subsequently, we must let go of our thoughts
and then connect with our feelings to begin the process.
During the process of surrender and release, we must focus
on how we are letting go, be aware of the depth of our
surrender and release of our feelings, recognize our limitations
of surrender and allow, permit the physiology of release to
take place. We must be conscious and respect our physiological
limitations at any given time. We acquire knowledge of
physiological limitations of surrender through our practice. The
release needs to be a thoughtful one that allows and permits
our success.

Stop Dwelling on Distress and Surrender

In the USA there is a tendency to dwell on distress. Often I hear
the cliché "Stop dwelling on your distress." This can mean several
things. It can mean the distress, the feelings are still present and
require additional surrender and release, or it can mean that the
person has a pattern of dwelling on distress. In either case both are
hurts and possibly trauma and need and require the emotional
space and time to experience a process.

Physical Surrender

The body can give us physical signals of what we need to surrender.
We can experience pain in certain parts of our body. We can use
bioenergetic exercises as a catalyst to help facilitate a process. The
bioenergetic exercises help us create the emotional space to allow
and to permit our connection with emotions. The exercises also
help us in the release of our feelings. We can use different body
movements to help us deceive control mechanisms that prevent us
from surrendering and releasing.

Soulful Surrender

This is sweet surrender. The tears flow in a loving, tender way. There is no struggle but a "giving up" and a tender release follows. The tears flow like a gentle loving rain that descends from the eyes effortlessly. The tears flow endlessly like the waterfall from the mountain into the lake or river without end. They are the tears of bliss. The tears nurture our nature and nurture that part of the self previously harboring the shadow and dark feelings. Here we connect with and begin to *feel* the infinite spiritual light entering our souls. Here we connect and give depth, degree, and dimension to our emotional surrender and release. Then we begin to feel the peace, the harmony, the beauty, and the tranquility of the infinite divine spark, *la chispa divina*. How sweet it is!

Heartfelt Surrender

True surrender must also come from the heart and felt in the heart to resolve issues such as shame and guilt. When two or more individuals hurt each other there must be a genuine giving and receiving of a heartfelt forgiveness in order to resolve pain energy. When two people resolve the pain energy in their hearts it facilitates forgiveness for and to each other. They can succeed through tools/methods individually, together, in group or perhaps use both or all methods to resolve issues. We must use our methods/tools to focus effectively and efficiently in order to learn how to let go of the range and nuances of our emotions to free ourselves from any pain within our heart. I believe this to be the prerequisite to spiritual surrender.

Spiritual Surrender

When one allows and permits surrender, the outcome is a deeper more profound connection with the universal divine spark occurring within and without. I believe it is here where we experience the connection with profound self and infinite spiritual love.

Intellectual Surrender

Get out of your head and be in your body. We say we won't allow our thoughts, our intellectualism to get in our way, to prevent us from connecting with our feelings, opening our hearts, and then to proceed to let go and release.

We use our intellect to facilitate our thinking, focus our process so that we are effective, efficient, and successful. We are intermittently thinking as we process our unhealthy energies. What is it that we need to think about now in order to facilitate our surrender? Are we ready to access certain emotions? Do we need to contradict those emotionally disturbing feelings with positive affirmations? Do we need to use bioenergetic exercises? Do we need to play spiritual music? As we instantaneously surrender and release energies automatically we are thinking of where more energies exist for us to address. There are messages that come to us as we surrender. We maintain our alertness to their callings. These are some of the concerns.

Creative Surrender

Surrender can become an art form by allowing and permitting ourselves to use our creativity. We can use positive affirmations to contradict our fears, anger, and sadness. When we use a positive tone and posture with an affirmation (use of the mirror as well), this attitude contradicts our negative or disturbing feelings, and this attitude becomes a catalyst in helping us help ourselves manifest emotional release.

An Infinite Calling to and of Surrender

The *soul* calls out to us through our cognitive and our intuitive bodies to cross whatever bridges exist in order for us to release those feelings that impact and do not resonate with our natures.

Decision to Surrender

I have found it necessary to have to make a cognitive decision to surrender. The mind and the body must be *ready* to release feelings associated with emotional shadow and darkness.

Intention to Surrender

There must be an intention of surrender. A mental, emotional, and physical attitude of intention is present.

Willingness to Surrender

We are lost without a willingness to surrender. Our will plays an essential part in our liberation. We must be emotionally open to the life force called "our will." We do this by receiving support. We ask support from our divine self, supportive individuals, other supportive elements that resonate with us. This could be music and/or significant items that have loving meaning in our lives. We need most of all support from our spiritual power outside ourselves. It is this spiritual power that helps us help ourselves when we feel we cannot go any further.

We can ask for spiritual help through prayer. We must be willing to ask, and we must be willing to be open to receive our divine powers messages. This will help us to surrender. It is here where the answers will come to us. Willingness creates a pattern of surrender. After we develop the pattern all the steps come instantaneously to us, and we accomplish the steps unconsciously. The steps become second nature.

Wanting Surrender

We succeed by being persistent, patient, and wanting to surrender our feelings. I want to experience a sense of freedom in my mind and my emotional body now. This is an attitude that must be present before we can succeed at releasing both suppressed and repressed feelings. It is those feelings that inhibit and imprison our emotional body and therefore our mind. We endow this attitude with empathy and compassionate love.

Authenticity of Surrender

Practice can make perfect. The authenticity of my own surrender has come with practice. The bioenergetic exercises have helped me to prepare my body for the physiology of emotional release. The exercises have helped me to create the emotional space to allow and permit the feelings to flow. I don't have to struggle to release my feelings after the emotional energy has been gone into and through. Surrender comes naturally.

Need to Surrender

There is a clear indication that all humankind has a consistent need to surrender. We tend to consistently be in denial of this need but it's the nature of our natures and the consistent calling of our beings to be free of any and all distress in our emotional bodies. The tensions within for many of us are just too great to *deny* ourselves the human expression of those feelings that call out for release.

Desire to Surrender

We must have a real, authentic desire to surrender. The desire to do the work must be present. I believe the desire for surrender comes from our heart center. I must connect with that *compassionate* heart center which facilitates, allows, and permits my emotional release.

Acting "As If" to Surrender

The authenticity of surrender may come when we act as if we are going to surrender. Fear is our barrier that prevents us from authentically feeling our feelings which upon their release we experience *truth* and *authenticity*.

Acting to Surrender

We must act to surrender. It isn't always easy to act to surrender. Our socialization process in society, defense mechanisms, beliefs, internalized judgments (what we think), and externalized judgments (what others think) gets in the way.

The Energy of Surrender

Uncovering Our Life Force: There is a so-called getting it. When we succeed in our surrender, we connect with more of our energy of essence. We learn to surrender our defenses. Freud's theory of psychoanalysis speaks to and about surrendering these walls. Our defenses according to Freud are our tendency to regress, rationalize, identify, deny, project, and displace. We learn to tap into our life force as we surrender and release our feelings reflective of distressful defensive patterns and their emotions. We release thoughts and feelings reflective of (anger, fear, and sadness) emotions that do not serve our well-being that reflect the above defenses. These obstructions have cognitive, emotional, and physical ramifications. We become more emotionally secure as we succeed. As we gradually do away with defenses and defense mechanisms, we reintegrate more of ourselves. We experience expansion and evolution of the self. Above all the result of our success is to intensify our self-acceptance and love.

Lightening Up Brings Effortless Surrender

Whatever is within that requires surrender can be connected to and released by lightening up in attitude. This can be accomplished through animated laughter. This is absolutely the best form in my opinion of the manifestation of release.

Effortlessness of Surrender

Depending on the issue that one is connecting to, going into, and going through, one may experience effortlessness of surrender. It's usually dependent upon how in touch one is with their range of feelings.

If one is readily open to one's feelings then surrender can be experienced in an effortless manner.

Effortful Surrender

If one is connecting to, going into and through walls of trauma then surrender can be experienced with effort.

Bioenergetic exercises, support from others, participating in a group experience can either open the necessary door to surrender or another catalyst may be in order to facilitate the process.

We do whatever it takes to succeed at and in the process of surrender in order to facilitate our release.

Knowing Primal and Primordial Surrender

This is the profoundest of emotional releases. I don't know of any deeper or more profound emotional release than the primal and primordial sounds of human sounds emanating from feelings of hurt and trauma. This is the most liberating of all experiences reflective of the most compassionate of self-healing experiences. This is especially true when there is someone in assistance and someone offering loving support while an individual is experiencing release.

True surrender
Opens the heart,
Awakens the spirit,
Cleanses the soul,
Strengthens the character,
And
Embraces the spirit.

Wisdom comes because of surrender!
The integration of total personality and spiritual aspects!
Breathe in the *love*
Breathe on out the *pain*
Let my heart be a place where this world is changed forever.
There is a way my spirit can pray
For the peace of everyone
With every breath I take my heart is learning to make
The will of love be done.

© 2003 by Inner Harmony Music
Words and music by Michael Stillwater

Permitting and Allowing the Suppressed and Repressed Feelings of Surrender to Release

Going into the Feelings

We begin to go into the feelings of sadness, anger, and fear. Then we resort to the courage that lies within the confines of the heart chakra. Then the heart chakra functions as a significant component where we allow its energy to move us ahead in the direction of feelings that we need to feel in order to achieve the transformational healing. We exercise our willingness, permitting and allowing ourselves to feel our feelings and the manifestations of release can be found. We usually find it necessary to create emotional space to feel our feelings. We're overwhelmed emotionally at times by demands, pressures, feelings, and responsibilities. We experience emotional shutdown. We need to create emotional space so that we can connect with our feelings. We can use the bioenergetic exercises to accomplish this task.

Going into the feelings is different from emotional release. We can be experiencing emotional release but not necessarily going into that space where the feelings are located. The key is to go into that space where the emotional energy of pain is present.

Going Through

We begin to go through the feelings, the range of the feelings reflective of a hurt or trauma. We go through the range of feelings— anger through rage, sadness through grief, fear through terror— their nuances, depths, degrees, and dimensions of time and space that has occluded, absorbed into, and integrated into our emotional bodies. When we experienced a hurtful or traumatic experience, a cloud formed within. If we don't release the energy of pain then it could cloud our emotional self and inhibit our flexible intelligence. It is this energy that remains and accumulates in our emotional body in the form of shadow and darkness. We become less aware, less alert, and have less attention for the world.

Follow-Through of Surrender

It's important to follow up on our work. The feelings reflective of our patterns can be triggered again so follow-up is almost automatic and necessary. It is always necessary to follow up on the follow-up until we sense that transformation has occurred.

Surrender of Tensions

We don't know where our tensions come from but they truly behoove us to address them by using our methods/tools.

Follow-Up of Surrender

Is there ever an end to these feelings? True transformation takes *work* and *time* dependent upon what pattern one addresses and how badly one has been hurt and traumatized.

Receiving Support to Surrender

The support that one receives that facilitates our surrender is a key component in making the whole process work! The chief component of that support is our sense of compassionate, empathetic love. This element of support *is* the cutting edge of *all healing, consciousness rising, liberation, enlightenment, and spiritual empowerment.* Support can come in many forms and shapes. The key to support is to receive the support one needs. Asking for support can be a challenge as well. We must be alert to our inhibitions that may consist of our beliefs, socialization processes, defenses, and defense mechanisms. The one feeling that always seems to get in the way is our *fear.* There could be many reasons for our fear. We can be afraid of being hurt again. The hurt may take the form of triggered feelings of fear reflective of rejection. We need to gradually learn to approach and *get through fear* and do whatever it takes to process it. This is the cornerstone of transformation.

Support can come from many door openers to surrender and release. "Empathy" is defined as the ability to see a situation from another person's point of view. It could come from a peer cocounselor who offers a touch, eye contact, or intuitive human connection, or it can be focused, attentive, aware, intelligent listening.

Empathy opens the door to compassion by providing a deeper emotional understanding of the individual's inner conflict. Being compassionate allows for the deliberate choice of an assertive response to resolving conflict within us and with others. It is the conduit for surrender. The empathy can take different forms of beauty, the beauty of nature, music, exercise, play; forms of relaxation, other healing art methods (please refer to the first book *I Dare to Heal with Compassionate Love.*)

The Joy and Enthusiasm of Surrender

We maintain a positive attitude and negotiate our surrender of unwanted emotion as we accumulate experience. We learn to pace ourselves and take the time we need until we succeed at our transformation. We learn to experience a joy and enthusiasm for surrender because in doing so we are motivated to make healthier lifestyle choices.

True Surrender

True surrender
True surrender
Faith is found, fear is shed
Faith is found, fear is shed
True surrender
True surrender

Fear is shed and love is found
More and more and more . . .

Love is found, love is found.

Points to Ponder:

Are you willing to make the commitment to yourself to initiate the components of surrender?

Can you benefit by learning emotional manifestations of the process?

Can you envision profound transformation of yourself because of your efforts?

CHAPTER 22

Release

Methods of Release

We use the methods of release that resonate with ourselves. We develop a treasure chest of methods and tools that nurture *our* nature. We must have a chest of tools and methods in hand that we can depend upon. We use our go-to tools if and when our patterns of distress are triggered. If and when we experience a knee jerk reaction that causes a disconnection between our mind and our body, our thoughts and our feelings, a distress or distresses that causes us to feel a sense of separation, abandonment, and betrayal within. We just plainly stop feeling like ourselves. The triggered knee jerk reactions are different for each of us because our experiences are all different from each other. How each of us reacts to our experiences, situations, and circumstances can be different as well. The reason again is that our individual genetic, biological, developmental, and the way we experience our hurt and traumas are different and unique.

I described many methods/tools in *I Dare to Heal with Compassionate Love*. Some of those examples include meditation, Viniyoga (yoga of the breath), Iyengar Yoga, counseling methods, dyad, mirror work, peer counseling, affirmations, Shiatsu, acupuncture, kinesiology, chiropractic, Tai Chi Chuan forms, taekwondo, primal primordial sound, devotional singing, drumming, and reflexology. I'll use as an example the integrated connected circular transformational divine healing breath. This breath has many names such as Rebirthing Breath, Holotropic Breath, Ecstasy Breathing, and Kundalini Yoga.

If the Eyes Don't Weep, Then Other Organs of the Body Will

The organs will hurt and become diseased. This is the reason humankind must, for their own and each others' well-beings, learn the manifestations of human release (in any manifestation of their choice that resonates with themselves) sufficiently to experience healing, personal growth, and spiritual power.

I use the integrated, expanding, evolutionary, transformational, divine, healing, circular, connected breath to surrender and release feelings that are reflective of shadow and darkness.

I pull in oxygen, connect, go into, go through the feelings, and upon the exhale, I release and emotionally let go of the feelings. The feelings are manifested in every way, shape or form possible. I feel the emotional dimensions of the feelings whatever and wherever they may be. I learned this method over a period of time in a gradual way. I began to learn how to negotiate my feelings associated with issues many years ago through peer cocounseling. If I encounter feelings associated with frozen need I use bioenergetic exercises to create emotional spaces for their access. This method is particularly effective when feeling paralyzing terror!

When we begin to go through the levels of feelings, a profound physiological need occurs for the feeling to move or emote from the body. When we go through the levels of feelings, the energy within begins to accumulate, and we create an emotional need for release. There is a need to move the energy out of our body. An analogy would be the swimmer stroking through the water. With each stroke he/she creates the accumulated energy that creates the forward motion. The moving down stroke of his hand connects with, goes into, and goes through the water. He creates an energy that is released, and the result is a motion forward through the water. It's a continuous circular movement with his hands and arms and his movement is always forward. We set in motion (emotionally) the feeling, and there is a natural need to let go or release. We feel a sense of joy and relief upon discharging that stored-up, restimulated, triggered, and knee-jerked unnecessary energy. We feel a sense of our own salvation. Most of all we feel a sense of peace as the feelings flow from us, and we experience a rebirth and connection with the divine universal spirit. This song is a reflection of the spirituality that results in this process.

Spirit Is Here with You

Spirit is here with *you.*
Spirit is holding *you.*
Spirit is loving *you* right now.

Spirit is here with you right now.
Spirit is holding you right now.
Spirit is loving you right now.

What is real is the love that we *feel.*
The love that is real.
The love that heals.
It's love that heals.

What is real is the love that we extend.
The love that never ends.
The love we feel within.
Spirit is here with us.

Spirit is holding us.
Spirit is loving us right now.
Loving *us* right Now.

Rhythms of Our Individualized Breath

Each of us has our *unique* rhythms of breath to connect with and release our toxic feelings. This is a learning process. We learn the rhythms of breath that best serve us to connect with and release toxic emotions. We need to have patience, persistence, and perseverance, support in learning our *unique* individualized rhythms of circular breathing. So we encounter a need for our release of feelings. We are automatically, by second nature, dependent on circumstances, situations, leading to *that* type and nature of breathing, connection, and release we *need*! We develop different rhythms of breathing to connect with toxic feelings. This takes practice and is fun to do. The more we practice different rhythms of our breath, the more comfortable and secure we become. We learn what rhythms of breathing best serve us and our connection to our toxic feelings and their release. The cliché "practice makes perfect" is correct. The more we practice different rhythms of our breath, the easier it is for us to learn the circular connection and nature of releasing our toxic feelings.

Circular Flow

We have found rhythms of circular breathing that work for us. Our rhythms help us to connect with, go into, and go through the levels of feelings that are triggered or restimulated within us. The exhale always has the impact of releasing those feelings. We have complete control over the depth, the degree, the emotional dimension of the connection with our emotions by the conscious decision of regulating the rhythms of our breath. Our breath can be deeper or shallower at times but always the connection of mind/body, cognitive/emotional, spirit/spiritual is present. Our practice is circular breathing daily so that it becomes second nature and always leaves us relaxed. I'm a substitute teacher on-call with adult and children presently so I experience a good deal of stress. I don't know if and when I'll be called by a school to work, nor the community where the school is located, nor the school I'll be going to in that community, nor the administration at the school, nor the parents of the children, nor the district I'll be working for, nor the children I'll be teaching, nor the system of the absent teacher. However, I live in faith.

The circular breath helps me to relieve that stress. I allow my stomach muscles to pull air into my body until my stomach inflates to the maximum and in doing so I connect with my feelings. I connect with daily stress or suppressed feelings / coiled energies / plumed serpents / the so-called underworld, a term from literature or simply repressed emotions. It is known as the lower world of emotions. The emotions housed in the rooted or pelvic chakra. I make the cognitive and emotional connection as I use my stomach muscles to pull oxygen into the pelvic area of my abdomen where I make the body-mind connection. I then allow and permit myself to surrender and release the feelings. I permit and allow any manifestations of release to take place. The mind-body connection is physiologically a natural one, and therefore, the body at any given circular breath innately knows what it needs to surrender and release.

The release or exhale is similar to a sigh. The manifestations of release can include primal, primordial sound; hot, cold sweats; tears; shaking; scratching; chattering; and sudden anger outburst with my fists; animated (with feelings) laughter; active kidneys; intermittent yawns. I've learned to feel safe when the onset of these manifestations result! I've learned to allow and permit the manifestations of release to happen. I've learned over and in time how to effectively and efficiently deceive thought or body controls that inhibit my awareness of addressing, accessing, going into, and going through surrendering and releasing any level of emotion. With each circular breath comes the surrender and release of raw energy. The primal and primordial sounds are not emotional releases but are concurrent or help to initiate emotional release. Newborn babies do this naturally. Socialization inhibits us from naturally doing this in our lives. Just think how resilient to stress and distress your life would be upon reeducating your self with the knowledge of release! We become less afraid to act upon our own behalf, to make mistakes.

Manifestations of Release

There are many manifestations of release as mentioned with *breathwork*. These forms of release become second nature. We begin to feel better subsequent to our release of these feelings.

The emotion that revolves is in revolution of the shadows and dark energies. They are many times wavelike, electric, storm filled, thunder filled, and lightinglike in composition. The energies are upward in movement and are eclectic, like the plumed serpents uncoiling their bodies similar to those energies in the ancient city and valley of the pyramids, Teotihuacan, Mexico.

The energies that are released are reflective of a range of feelings that consists of angers through rage, sadness through grief, and the most resistant, reluctant, and frustrating of feelings of energies to awaken, i.e., the fear through terror and all its emotional depths, degrees, levels, and emotional dimensions. With the revolving energies upward comes the *empowerment and the integrative consciousness of the self*. With the empowerment of the components and facets of the self comes the expansion, the evolution, the recreation, the rebirth, and reintegration and a holotropic result of a movement toward the one, the complete *holy and whole* self. It is along the way and it is here at the apex of the pyramid where we connect with our inner spiritual self and our universal spiritual power.

Keeping Calm

One cannot help but to choose calm, calm, calm
meaning deeply reaches.

Keeping calm in the experience of a connection, surrender, and release of emotion comes at the culmination of release of the feelings.

Keeping calm in the experience of release requires learning self-discipline. We learn to keep calm when not experiencing the surrender and release of our feelings.

Happy and Whole

Happy and whole, healthy and free
With each breath that I breathe
The more I let go
The more I receive
And feel peace inside of me
For I am one with the breath
of life.
Like the sun shining oh so bright.
I am one with the breath of life.
Like the sun shining.

© 2002 by Malaya Rider
All rights reserved.

Points to Ponder:

Have you ever experienced any manifestations of emotional release?
How could the experience of emotional release aid you in your healing, your personal growth?
Have you ever observed anyone experiencing manifestations of emotional release?
What were your reactions?
Can you imagine how emotional release can contribute to the enhancement of your spiritual power?

CHAPER 23

Doing It Enough

Nightmares

When I opened Pandora's Box I became haunted by
waves of emotion; they were reflective of the colors
of the rainbow, pictures that were quite grotesque,
and rays of light emanating through shadow and
darkness; they were represented by snapshots and
photos of my collected unconscious.

These are experiences that others have shared with me using methods
of effective circular breath and emotional release.

Jane

I dreamt a lion had gotten out of its cage, and it was attacking my
friend. The lion was injured and lay near its cage with a bleeding
limb. My friend was very compassionate and ran immediately to
its aid. I watched, thinking my friend was insane to go to aid an
injured lion. After all how would the injured lion react? Well, the
lion jumped at my friend with its long hair waving in the wind
and its teeth ready to devour the head of my buddy. I was paralyzed
with terror and didn't know what to do. I looked around for a stick
or rock to scare off the animal but that was just an afterthought.
The lion was ready to put his long teeth into the skull and neck of
my friend. Suddenly the lion backed off and returned to its cage
leaving my friend uninjured. My friend decided once again to go
near the broken cage door, and this time two lions broke out of the

same cage, smashing down the entrance. This time my friend didn't seem as lucky, but my dream ended right then and there without conclusion. I was in sheer terror and paralyzed not knowing what to do.

I awoke out of the dream feeling very tensed and decided to do the circular connected breath. The breath allowed me to move into the emotional space within where I held the tension of terror and begin to release it. I became the buddy and the friend one in the same, and I gradually dissipated the terror of the nightmare. The manifestations of release were primal and primordial sound and animated laughter.

We have nightmares that emanate from our consciousness. It is our choice to look and address the feelings reflective of our emotions. If and when we address enough of our feelings, we can discover more peace, joy, and happiness within. We can also discover the reasons for our nightmares.

Agitation

*The choice was clear; I discharged my underlying
feelings of fear and anger.*

David

I can become quite agitated for a variety of reasons. I all too often have little control over our situations and circumstances so we can choose to persevere until the feelings hopefully dissipate. I can address our agitation (inner self-directed frustration, anger, and fear) once again with the use of the circular, connected, healing breath.

I have been consistently underemployed and unemployed and negotiate my feelings of frustration through the circular breath. The following is an example of the emotional release of agitation.

I became so itchy that I couldn't help but to begin scratching. The frustrated feelings permeated my skin, and I just needed to remove it with my fingernails. I continued to breathe and access my feelings, and they continued to surface through my skin. I couldn't stop scratching myself.

After all agitation is like having a severe inner itch rising to the surface. The animated laughter, scratching, primal and primordial sounds released again and again helped to dissipate the feelings of frustration and inner self-directed anger. The severe itch dissipated, and I was able to direct my energies differently by focusing on constructive tasks.

Consciousness Raising

FRED

I have often been stressed out when driving in Los Angeles traffic jams. It's very tedious to be stuck in traffic jams. I clear my brain and return to being alert by yawning. I release the stress through the yawn. I feel invigorated after releasing the tension.

I experience a great deal of tension when I'm in large crowds. Recently, I attended the Los Angeles Times Festival of the Book. The attendance of the festival was estimated to be 170,000 people over a two-day period. I was very tensed walking around the University of California campus attempting to locate specific booths. I lay down on the grass and practiced accessing and releasing my feelings of tension by way of yawning. The yawn was reflective of a profound release of energy. I felt completely invigorated. The inhale was very deep, and the yawns were very long exhales. I released enormous tension.

Karen

I applied for an advanced degree over a two-year period to a program. I took additional classes as prerequisites for the school. I truly wanted to return to school! The competition was stiff, but I felt I had a good chance of being accepted. I failed on three occasions to be accepted to the program. I experienced depression. I used the effectiveness of a variety of methods to surrender and release a range of feelings, including sadness through grief reflective of my discouragement. I experienced a sense of peace and liberation from the sadness because of my ability to let go. I continue to seek other ways so I can return to school and continue my studies.

Enthusiasm

The attitude is enthusiastic regardless of the tool/method used to address feelings reflective of emotion. The enthusiasm is significant in helping us to help ourselves surrender and release stuck, suppressed, and repressed feelings.

Again and Again and Again

The process of again, again, and again—repeating the surrender and release of the feelings—is absolutely necessary in moving whatever negative feelings existing within. We have so-called restimulation of past hurtful and traumatizing feelings from the bumps, potholes, dips, and craters in our lives.

We are impacted differently by the nature of stress and distress. We can experience a trauma differently from how others experience exactly the same trauma. We may experience the energy of pain where other individuals may not experience the same energy of pain from having the same experiences. The reason is we are different. Our genetic, biological, developmental, and environmental makeup are different, and this reflects our sensitivities, temperaments, and personalities.

We can use spiritual music to aid in surrendering and releasing of our feelings. The music helps to relax us in a gentle, loving way so that we can begin to access the feelings reflective of the emotions in our body. The music helps us to release the feelings and move once again into the inhale portion of the circular breath.

Is It Ever Enough?

It depends upon the depth, degree, and dimension of the nuances of the emotional or physical hurt or trauma! It depends upon the depth and degree of our courage/tenacity to feel through and surrender and release our feelings. Are we mentally and physiologically ready in the process of our mind/body connection? Do we have the loving support of at least one individual who can be there for us? We then gradually develop the courage/tenacity to dare to heal with our spiritual power and naturally develop the maturity of surrender and release. We experience the wonder of personal and spiritual growth in our lives. It is in essence a spiritual process but above all a human one!

Doing It Enough

The key is to be able to liberate ourselves. Are we able to let go of "enough" of the triggered and restimulated feelings. The key is to release *enough* of the range of feelings, anger through rage, fear through terror, and sadness through grief. We release the ranges of emotional nuances, depths, degrees, and most importantly, the emotional dimensions of the feelings of distress and trauma. The emotions reflective of our issues, unhealthy patterns of behaviors, wounds, potholes, bumps, craters, and dips in our lives. It is those inhibiting rigid feelings that we have ignored. We have ignored them because we have consciously or unconsciously been hurt and have chosen not to look at them!

Isaac Newton, the master of physics, describes motion, space, and time. This is also true of the emotional body. The word "motion" is contained in the word "emotion." Distress and stress, our patterns occupies emotional space and limits our emotional time in shadow and darkness. We free up the emotional space which gives us a sense of more emotional time, and we liberate significant space that was previously occupied by distress. This is replaced by light. The light increases in the eyes of the individual and can be readily seen by others. The eyes are truly the windows to the spirit and the soul!

We can actually feel the different range of emotion as we engage in the practice of circular breathing. As we experience enough of the release of feelings at different depths, degrees, and dimensions, our transformation and integration of ourselves materializes. We have increased our emotional quotient, cognitive intelligence, acquired more attention for the world, and more importantly we have become more empathetic, compassionate, and loving!

Points to Ponder:

Do you have the enthusiasm to look at your memories and address both suppressed and repressed emotions?

Is the transformational breath process a possible tool/method that you could possibly use to expedite your personal and spiritual growth?

Do you have the willingness to address the inner frontier of the self?

Do you ever experience nightmares or periods of agitation?

Are you mentally and emotionally ready to permit and allow yourself to address your conscious and dormant emotions?

Are you willing to create the time to do so?

Can you possibly conceive of greater happiness in your life through raising your consciousness?

CHAPTER 24

Your Spiritual Power, You Own It

Humility, Forgiveness, Grace, Redemption, Gratitude,
Liberation, Zest, Unconditional Love, Consideration
for Others

We will become one world nation that is in possession of their spiritual power and is living a life filled with divine zest!

Arab peoples are coming to know their own spiritual power because of their liberation by coalition forces. Their consciousness is hopefully being raised because of the liberation of Iraq! This is certainly a period of transition for the people of the Middle East. It holds great promise for the future. However, the reality just now is that some Middle Eastern people are experiencing a sense of humiliation because of foreign forces occupying Iraq. I take a Western point of view regarding their humiliation. I see their anger as a transitional consciousness raising period. People are learning to take responsibility for their own lives in their own countries. This requires education and it's a gradual process. The people in the Middle East have known only dictatorship. This has been their mind-set! The result of this mind-set is to foster a so-called holy war terrorism against the coalition forces. This will gradually dissipate as more people experience political, economic, educational, and emotional empowerment. There are too many dictators in the Middle East that exploit the presence of the occupying coalition as a form of humiliation. There are too many religious schools that foster radical, educational doctrines that reinforce hatred for the West—Christian and Jewish people. The Madrases teach that Christians/Jews are conspirators in the world, and they are not to be trusted! The Madras's creates radical Islamic thinking and groups committed to violence, hatred, and exploitation! The dictatorships are in fact frightened of the democratic forces that may come to bear in this region. The dictators are afraid of losing power and control over their people.

The Iraqi army that was disbanded and many young Iraqis who were members of the military carry a great deal of anger. The insurgents in Iraq, the Baath party, and other groups exploit the feelings of the discontented Iraqi people to foster their own self-interest. They use fear and intimidation to prevent transition. They exploit the feelings of frustration and anger and the conditions of poverty and scarcity in order to ferment turmoil. The radicals are desperately frightened of losing control as well! It can only help when grievances are acknowledged, anger listened to, and actions taken to contradict these radical forces. This will take time and patient persistence, perseverance, material, and sadly, human sacrifice on the part of peoples of the world. People need to be listened to in order to expedite the process of nation building. The priority for the present is creating a sense of security in the country of Iraq. Sovereignty creates the beginning of spiritual empowerment for the people of Iraq.

It's Human to Err, It's Divine to Forgive

From the 1930s film *Intermezzo* with Ingrid Bergman.

Self-Forgiveness

When we truly forgive then we know that what has transpired by hurt and trauma has never happened! It is then we have thoroughly let go of the pain! Then it becomes a painless memory!

Forgiveness is harbored in our heart chakra. We are not victims but feel like victims. We have our losses and our resulting feelings of human emotion in our lives. We experience the depths, degrees, and dimensions of these ranges of feelings.

We just don't have control over others, and we learn soon that it's our own insecurity within that creates a tendency for us to control others' behaviors. We experience loss because of divorce, relationships, children, employment, and rejection from friends, family, schools, and deaths of loved ones. How do we cope? Surrendering and releasing our feelings that don't serve us free us from the energy of our pain. It is in taking charge and becoming a proactive being we experience "eternal sunshine and maintain a spotless mind" as is indicated by a recent film title. As we experience self-forgivingness and forgiveness of others, we forgive ourselves.

We experience self-forgivingness and forgivingness of others through our ability to surrender and release enough of our fears, angers, and sadness. If and when we release enough of our fears, we realize a new state of consciousness. The realization is that the hurt/trauma never happened. We are left with the memory without the pain. Fear can get in our way of experiencing self-forgivingness and forgivingness of others. It is in feeling through our fear again and again where we can achieve authentic forgivingness. Fear is our greatest barrier to our authentic selves and experiencing forgivingness.

Divine Grace and Forgiveness

The experience of emotional grace and forgiveness is sweet. We surrender and release our feelings as they reflect our emotions and can better experience our empathy and compassion for ourselves and/or others. We can then better experience a feeling of grace and forgiveness. We feel sweetness within our emotional body because of our experiencing a "forgivingness." The grace is divinely given to us because of our experience of forgiveness. We heal our spirit when we experience spiritual grace. We endow our spirit spiritually. We can experience the power of the so-called white light effect because of our acceptance of grace. The ability to receive grace is a natural inclination of human nature. Unproductive emotions are the barriers that prevent us from learning and receiving forgiveness and accepting grace within ourselves. We can either transcend or transform our unproductive emotions and experience spiritual grace.

Amazing Grace

Amazing grace
Pouring down on me.
(Repeated three times)

Amazing grace
Pouring down
When I surrender my will
And let your love care for me.

Amazing grace fills my life.
(Repeated twice)

© 2004 by Marsha Jeha
All rights reserved.

Touched by an Angel

I've been touched by an angel.
I've been touched by her healing grace.
Oh, I've been touched by an angel.
I've been touched by her grace.

When she sings with me, I open to harmony.
When I sing with her, I learn to be free.
When she sings with me, I open to harmony.
When I sing with her, I learn to be free.

I've been touched by an angel.
I've been touched by her healing grace.
Oh, I've been touched by an angel.
I've been touched by her grace.

When she sings with me, I open to harmony.
When I sing with her, I learn to be free.
When she sings with me, I open to harmony.
When I sing with her, I learn to be free.

We've been touched by the angels.
We've been touched by their healing grace.
Oh, we've been touched by the angels.
We've been touched by their grace.

When they sing with us, we open to harmony.
When we sing with them, we learn to be free.
When they sing with us, we open with harmony.
When we sing with them, we learn to be free.

We've been touched by the angels.
We've been touched by their healing grace.
We've been touched by the angels.
We've been touched by their grace.
We've been touched by their grace.

© 2002 by Malaya Rider

Gratitude

When we have experienced a sense of graceful feelings, spiritual
joy, then gratitude takes charge and an appreciation of what we
have in our lives occurs. Miracles happen when we take

responsibility and do the necessary work! The keys that open the door to grace and forgiveness are the following:

Doing the work!
Doing the work!
Doing the work!
Doing the work!

Redemption of Those Dark and Shadow Sides of Self

It is then that we experience a profound sense of redemption and peace within. It is here where we experience the removal of the emotional shadows and darkness. We experience the removal of those feelings that get in our way. When we emotionally process our feelings we create the bridge to our spirituality and to the spiritual connection to ourselves and to our spiritual being. We have arrived into the spiritual dimension of divine light. This experience enhances our self and our spiritual essence. We experience divine spiritual growth in and to our spiritual body.

We use our consciousness-raising tools and methods that resonate with ourselves and through our practices we experience spiritual power and enlightenment! The result of doing our work is to experience the illumination of the self and compassionate love! We remove the pain energy around our issues, and we are left with memories and divine personal power! We are also left we the zest of our liberation!

Liberation

The spiritual leader and song writer Cass Smith sings of "liberation" in Sanskrit with the song "Atma Vicharya." The chorus of the song is as follows:

ATMA VICHARYA

ATMA VAICHARYA, ATMA VAICHARYA,
ATMA VAICHARYA, "LIBERATION"
PURIFY THE MIND; PURIFY THE MIND,
   THROUGH SATVA JAPA MEDITATION.

PURIFY THE MIND; PURIFY THE MIND,
THROUGH SATVA JAPA MEDITATION.

ATMA VAICHARYA, ATMA VAICHARYA,
ATMA VAICHARYA, "LIBERATION."

Satva—meaning purity
Japa—meaning repetition of the name of God
Atma Vicharya—liberation, search for self, especially by the
   question, "Who am I?"

Consideration for Others

When we come to know liberation and zest, we do this in a
practical way by expressing gracefulness, unconditional love,
and refraining from taking issues personally when they arise. If
we do take it personally, then we can use our methods and
tools with focus, effectively and efficiently, to free ourselves
from the pain. We must respond to attacks by stating our
disagreements and then move on!

Unconditional Love and Learning Acceptance

We can learn to negotiate our emotions if and when we have taken
comments personally. We must realize that those comments impact

our self-acceptance. We learn to do this through a state of consciousness that requires an awareness of our emotional stress and/or distress experiences. If we need to surrender and release emotions in order to achieve self-acceptance, we can go to our methods and tools to expedite the surrender and release of feelings that have impacted us. We learn to integrate ourselves, learn self-acceptance, acceptance of others, and thereby learn unconditional love. This helps us to maintain and expand our liberation and peace of mind. The process can be a gradual one or it can be accomplished quite immediately. We can learn to process our upset emotions reflective of our feelings quickly. It is a process!

Reemergence (from the Hurt or Trauma)
Enlightenment (Reevaluation)
Follow-Up
Liberation
Follow Up on the Follow-Up
A Continued Connection and Sense of Liberation
Clarity
Self-Acceptance (Total Rejection of Self-Denial)
Leads to Healthier Thoughts, Feelings, Choices, Intentions,
Actions, Results, and Character.

Peace: The act of cleansing the tension using the circular, connected, conscious, expansive, evolutionary, healing, transformational, integrative, divine breath brings us immediate liberation and peace! This deep-seated circular breath brings instantaneous and immediate results.

The tension in our bodies can build up because of experiences of frustration for example. We can then completely release the frustration through the circular breath. The complete release results in profound emotional peace within. Behind the shadow and dark emotions reflective of our feelings lies emotional peace and tranquility. There is comfort and rest. We achieve the following:

HUMILITY, GIVING & RECEIVING,
TOLERANCE, BEAUTY, BLISS, JOY, LOVE,
FAITH, TRUST, SECURITY, HEALTH,
CELEBRATION, ENTHUSIASM, ANIMATED
OPEN EMOTIONAL EXPRESSION, ENGAGING
IN RELATIONSHIPS AND UNFOLDING
COMMUNITY, CREATIVITY, SPIRITUAL,
SOULFUL, INTELLECTUAL, EMOTIONAL
STABILITY, PHYSICAL, SPIRITUAL
ENLIGHTENMENT

Points to Ponder:

Can you envision the consciousness rising of suppressed, oppressed, and repressed people of the world emotionally as well as politically?

Have you ever experienced forgiveness, grace, and redemption of your self through the surrender and release of unproductive emotions?

Can you give gratitude for ten different items in your life today?

Can you envision your own liberation from shadow and dark feelings in your body reflective of strong emotion?

How do you handle situations where you have taken comments personally?

Can you envision unconditional love in relationship to family, friends, and acquaintances?

How would it be for you to experience authentic peace of mind, body, spirit, and soul?

CHAPTER 25

Journey to Marin

Danielle needed support. She needed to get away from her father. She had enough in her relationship with her dad. Danielle was a woman of about thirty-five years old with long brown hair, brown eyes, and light skin. She had many hobbies. Her most interesting of them was making bridges from toothpicks.

But now she had had enough of living with her alcoholic dad, and she was returning to Marin County, California. She owned an RV and asked me to follow her vehicle with her prized possession, i.e., her 1984 Chevrolet Corvette. I agreed and on a Tuesday morning, just prior to the New Year, we began our journey north from National City, California, to Marin County.

I had never been to Marin County before so this would be an adventure. We arrived in the RV park after a thirteen-hour drive, and I soon fell asleep in Danielle's recreational vehicle. I slept in her made-up bed from the kitchen table. In the ensuing days we visited Pt. Reyes, San Geronimo Valley, San Rafael, and the towns of Fairfax, Mill Valley, the Italian restaurant D'Angelo's, and the music pub Sweetwater, the Zen center in Green Gulch, Muir Beach, the spiritual center Spirit Rock, the towns of Sausalito, Tiburon, Corte Madera, and played with and walked Timothy the golden retriever in view of the San Quentin State Penitentiary.

Spirit Rock is a spiritual retreat just east of the town of Fairfax. It's nestled in the hills and valleys of Marin County. It follows in the teachings of the Buddhist tradition and offers programs to a wide variety of groups. I attended the 2004 New Year's Eve Celebration. The rain poured down as we celebrated the coming of the new year with spiritual meditation, music, song, dance, comedy, poetry, and food prepared especially for the occasion.

Spirit Rock's goal is to offer programs where the spiritual seeker is able to look inward and find more of those parts of themselves to help them embody more wisdom, peace, and compassion within. The staff at Spirit Rock hopes that participants will bring these qualities into the world in order to create authentic, positive transformation.

I attended a group meditation and lecture at the Zen center in Green Gulch. The center is a Buddhist retreat center that combines spiritual practice and management of surrounding land to foster environmental awareness and education. It is located in a secluded valley and surrounded by Mount Tamalpais State Park and the Marin County Water District. It is near beautifully secluded Muir Beach and is in easy walking distance from the Zen center. This was the first meditation of the New Year 2004, and it was particularly poignant because of the attendance of young children. The meditation focused on the use of the breath and how it is a wonderful catalyst for us to live in the present moment.

A Meditation

I invite you to get comfortable in your chair—feel the support of the floor under your feet, the chair supporting your body. Now follow your breath into your body. Just notice your stomach gently rising and falling as the smooth rhythm of your breath informs your mind and heart that you are about to enter into sacred time. As you follow your breath into the chamber of your heart allow your body to soften. Now allow your mind to focus on a recent commitment you have made with yourself or a desire that has not yet formed into a commitment. Now imagine that you are standing in a threshold, and allow your attention to be drawn to the past behind you. Notice all the things that have supported you—those things which have brought you to this very moment. Just observe it. No judgment. Just noticing. As you allow yourself to witness these old patterns and behaviors your heart begins to expand, and you allow yourself to sense a deep compassion for all that has been—to feel gratitude for the whole of your life right up to this moment: everything. And in this deep gratitude and compassion you begin to sense peace with all that is. This feeling of peace and gratitude has a transformational quality—an alchemical affect—and you feel yourself expanding, your awareness expanding, and you realize you are greater than any condition in your life, and this new wisdom invites you to look in front of you across the threshold toward what is waiting. Your commitment, your desire is right there before you—desired result, fully or order, glorious and resplendent in its fullness. Allow yourself to feel what you see as if it was so right now. Allow your heart to inform your mind that you have everything it takes to cross this threshold. Your whole life has prepared you for this moment. You are not stepping alone but with spirit to guide you through this alchemical portal—to fullness of your full beingness of expression.

Contributed by Candace Kienitz, RSCP
Religious Science Practitioner

Cancer Control Society

I was invited to the Cancer Control Society Conference held in Universal City, California, the end of August 2003 to display and present *I Dare to Heal with Compassionate Love*. The response from professionals and nonprofessionals was very positive. It seemed many participants at the conference just gravitated to the narrow corner of the author-signing table where I had the display. A select number of speakers spoke about the significance of oxygen as a healing component of disease. I wrote about breathing techniques for surrendering and releasing toxins from the body. It was my honor to bring this aspect of healing and the message of *I Dare to Heal with Compassionate Love* to the conference.

Emotionally upsetting feelings can have significant impact on the cells of the body. The message was by using the catalyst of the breath we can address, access, and connect with, go into, go through, surrender and release of both suppressed and repressed feelings. The accumulation of both repressed and suppressed feelings have profound unhealthy chemical changes within the genes in the cells of the body. The unhealthy chemical changes in the genes of the cells of the body can bring about disease physically, emotionally, and mentally. When we have the right intention and act successfully to surrender and release toxins from the cells of our bodies, we then have a healthy transformational impact on the genes. The chemical natures of our genes remain healthy, the cells of our body remain healthy, and our bodies remain healthy. There is the possibility of profound release of unhealthy toxins from the genes in our cells by way of learning and practicing deep, circular, rhythmic breathing patterns of breathing.

Points to Ponder:

Have you ever visited a spiritual retreat center?

What do you think can you gain from participating in a program at a spiritual retreat center?

Would a group you are associated with find it useful to experience a retreat at just such a center?

Do you think that significant emotion unreleased from your body is a contributing factor in the cause of cancer?

CHAPTER 26

The Cover

The cover of the book came about after interviewing several artists and finding one whom I resonated with and who resonated with me. The San Diego artist read through portions of the manuscript and became inspired by the story. He is both an artist and a musician. I think he is very talented and of course like all of us has his own personal issues, demons to struggle with and confront.

Randy Brown and I seemed to connect cognitively, emotionally, and spiritually. I knew immediately that he would be the chosen artist to depict and communicate best the message in the book. He is familiar with life's struggles. Randy is a man in his fifties, tall, perhaps 6'2", Caucasian, has strong features, and was an American veteran of the Vietnam War. I gave him the manuscript, and he read through portions of the book and became inspired by the message of healing, personal growth, and self-liberation. Randy took an artist's brush and oil and proceeded to do the cover.

The power of the book cover is spiritually inspiring. The covers of the books *I Dare to Heal with Spiritual Power* and *I Dare to Heal with Compassionate Love* contain great healing powers. Readers have often said that upon gazing at the cover they feel a great deal of peace and tranquility. The covers of the books are representative of a mantra! I agree with their observations. From the pain energy one has experienced in one's life can come healing, personal growth, and liberation. The struggle within us just seems to come to an end as one gazes at the cover and becomes one with peaceful contentment. It's like a gate we walk through or a mirror that reflects our peace, sense of security, and serenity.

As I gaze at the cover, my own attention focuses on the waterfalls, then the clouds, the snowcapped mountains, the trees of life, the shoreline with its rocks, and the interplay of colorful flowers with all of their intricate nuances. The three swans, one has his wings open and the others in the background with their wings closed. The swan is a symbol of transformation since they begin their lives in shades of gray and transform to the inevitable color of white, symbolic of spiritual light. There are the nuances of the lake and the play of colors—light, then dark shadows. The additional elements of the sky and its shades of red and white just seem to play in the painting. There are the clouds. There is the range of colors similar to the range of emotions reflective of feelings that I will discuss later. The colors of white, red, yellow, green. It's definitely springtime descending upon the earth. Please notice how the letters of the title and the letters of my name move from shadow and darkness in the background to white light. This is also a reflection of transformation. I usually say the cover represents a mirror to a human being. The mirror reflects the range of experiences that a human being encompasses throughout his whole life. There is the range of colors as there is the range of emotions reflective of human feelings. We experience the sadnesses, angers, fears, joys, insecurities, inadequacies, safety, security, love, peace, serenity. I've often imagined the cover to reflect the soul and spirit of a human being. The cover is just like a mirror reflecting the trials and tribulations of human experience, the emotional ups and downs, and struggle of relationships, spirit, and the soul.

I've asked potential readers to first "look at" the cover then to "look into" the cover. The reaction has always been different. I believe the cover represents a gate; a gate which, when you look into it, allows you to see the whole range of your life's experiences from birth, present, and perhaps future time. There is the presence of a timeless source ever present, everlasting.

We have an inner sanctuary of peace that we all can connect to and go to where we can find the experience of self-love. Once we have been reunited with our inner sanctuary of peace, we can intuitively and consciously go there when we need to. To know that regardless of your mistakes that you have always in all ways done the best taking "everything" into account in your life. The choices you have made though at times resulting in pain do not deserve self-reproach but self-understanding based on a present time newfound awareness that fosters an awakened sense of responsibility and forgiveness. We learn that we have always done our best and deserve no self-reproach and even reproach or invalidation from others.

The cover reminds me of a gate of life. The more we gaze at the cover we perhaps decide to move through it and experience the range of emotion. Do you dare experience these ranges of feelings reflective of those emotions? Do you dare address those emotional gaps and spaces that may exist between those feelings? The cover is enticing. It lures one into the darkness, the shadows, and yes, the light and renewal.

The shadows and darkness envelope our tenacity for healing and personal growth and most importantly our self-realization of our personal spiritual power.

Please focus on the clouds. Perhaps it was raining, the storm, the lightning and the thunder are so reflective of our own lives. One observer claimed that the clouds appeared to him as an eagle. We can have the experience of an eagle soaring! We may have experienced the emotional ups and downs, those dips, bumps, craters, and potholes in our lives. The experiences of stresses and the distresses: the insecurities, vulnerabilities, doubts, inadequacies, and reservations. We have those emotional and practical needs unmet and the frozen needs that have become known to us on an intuitive basis or perhaps reflective of our own behaviors. There may have been a storm of thunder and lightning reflective of internal conflict. This can be construed as being reflective of our screams, groans, and grunts that we may have felt and perhaps learned to surrender and release through sound.

Points to Ponder:

Have you looked at the cover of the book and have you looked into the cover of the book?

Does the cover of the book become a mirror to your soul?

Have you closed your eyes after observing the cover and looked inward?

Have you seen other book covers or pictures which have inspired you?

What is it that you like about the cover of the book?

What do you dislike?

CHAPTER 27

Life's Wish, Life's Dream, Life's Bliss
Peace Within!

I believe our "life's wish" is to find an authentic love for ourselves and in doing so we experience bliss, peace, joy, and satisfaction within our lives. We all have our human challenges within us. We all have those black holes containing enormous energy that can be transformed into enhancing our life wish. It is the power and energy of our shadow and darkness that gets in our way. It is through the same shadow and darkness that our hurts/traumas, dips, bumps, potholes, and craters in our life cause anxiety, fear, grief, doubt, reservation, insecurities and permeate our emotional and physical bodies. It is also through these shadow and dark places that we can find true self-love, bliss, peace, joy, and satisfaction. There is much that gets in the way of our self-realization. I speak more about this in chapter 5.

The more we work focused, effectively, and efficiently on our issues the more we grow into wholeness and fulfill our "life wish" within ourselves. The more whole and healthy human beings we are! The more we dare to heal with spiritual power because of surrender and release, the more we let go of our fears, angers, and grief and the more love, bliss, and joy we connect with and experience. The more peace we experience within. It is then when we come to know God and Godliness within and without. It's definitely what all humankind seeks whether humankind is cognitively aware of it or not! We seek spiritual love within! We gradually evolve, expand, and unfold until we experience authentic, divine love!

It can take but one good breath session where we have experienced profound surrender and release and then we experience authentic, divine love. We are then hooked into experiencing spiritual love again and again and again. We are hooked into experiencing divine bliss again and again and again. When our emotions/feelings are triggered once again it becomes easier to work in, through, and out our feelings until we experience thorough liberation of self. It is the nature of nature that energy which doesn't serve us is triggered again. It is that same energy that is a catalyst to humankind—an upward trend, whether we like it or not which leads to self-realization!

There are many in the world who falsely think and feel that they are living their life's desires and dreams and still somehow desire more in their lives. This is because energies that do not serve them lie dormant within their repressed emotional body. We all have life's challenges. Our challenges tend to be the nature of our life's wish itself. It's nature's contribution to developing our character and strengthening our bliss. It's nature's contribution telling us to appreciate what we have and therefore what we can expand to experience yet more! It's incumbent on us to do the inner work to awaken the love, bliss, peace, joy, and satisfaction. We must have the tenacity to do so. It does become easier after we have had but one good emotional surrender and release session. After we've had one good cry!

There are many in the world who have yet to rediscover themselves by focusing, effectively and efficiently, and exploring their inner frontiers. There are many who have yet to find so-called true fulfillment but yet dream of it and have a desire to do so. There are many who are confused about what in fact fulfillment is! There are many in the world who are struggling and striving to reach their bliss. *I Dare to Heal with Spiritual Power* is a book for all people wherever they are on their journey of life. The book encourages and challenges us to dare to transform those energies that get in our way of doing and manifesting our bliss. It is our decision that can help us to transform ourselves in a responsible way.

The process is a gradual one with many successes along its path. Patience, persistence, and the dynamic access to and connection with those energies reflective of pain and their surrender/release empower us to energize ourselves helping ourselves along the pathway by facilitating, enlightening, and deepening our conscious behaviors. We become conscious human beings. We are conscious of our inadequacies and insecurities and better able to address them effectively. We become conscious of those rediscovered parts of ourselves that were formally in shadow and darkness and now experience light, love, bliss, peace, joy, and satisfaction. The more we nourish ourselves by productively working from within and releasing from within, the more we experience our life wish expanding and evolving. The more of nature's nourishment we experience, the more we enjoy our relationships with family, friends, and co-workers. It's the nature of humankind. It's the natural progression of nature within and around us. It's like the claim of the "transcendentalists" that what we really are looking for is our unity with God.

The more we focus on the positive and good in our lives, the more our emotion and feelings of stress and distress will bubble up from suppressed and repressed emotion. It is incumbent on us to address whatever feelings arise. The more we transform the negative and bad in our lives by learning to release our emotional shadows and darkness, the more profound our life wish becomes. The more we can take charge of our worlds in relationship to others in and of our environment. The result is greater life and spiritual energy that we connect with and the greater life and spiritual energy we experience in a loving way with each other. "Chain Reaction" by songwriter Steve Ducey expresses the natural force of nature to move us into wholeness and fulfill our life's dream and life's bliss both in a practical and spiritual way.

Chain Reaction

I was a child
Dreamed of who'd I be
It was a vision of my destiny
But with time it failed
Self-doubt prevailed

I went to school
And learned a trade
I chose my life's work
Based on what it paid
I climbed the ladder
But nothin' mattered

I heard a voice inside me sayin'
"Live up to your dream"
That voice grew louder
Until it was a scream
"If you don't heed this warning
Fearing all that you might lose
The life that you were born for
Will not be there to choose"

So I took a chance
Stumbled in the dark
I climbed a trail
That wasn't marked
Oh, I got lost
But I found my heart

As I climbed that path
I began to sow
The seeds of purpose
That passion grows
That dream inside me
Was for reviving my soul

That voice inside kept sayin'
"Live up to your dreams"
It took me half a lifetime
To remember what that means
When we fold our aspirations
Like a poker hand that's bad
We never get to see the life
We know we should've had

When you leave behind
All your doubts and fear
Your life's purpose suddenly appears
When you chase your passion
There's a chain reaction
Your dreams become real
They become real.

Written by Steve Ducey
© 2001 by Falling Awake Music (ASCAP)

Points to Ponder:

Are you ready to accept your passion and discover more love, joy, bliss, satisfaction, and peace of mind in your life?

Are you conscious that your passion has its ups and downs, its successes and disappointments, its victories and defeats?

Are you resilient?

Are you willing to explore your inner emotional frontiers and do what it takes to develop resiliency?

Are you willing to strive for more authenticity with yourself and in your relationships?

Are you willing to be patient, persistent, persevering, and develop the self-disciplines to succeed on your pathway and dare to heal with spiritual power?

GLOSSARY

Bioenergetics:* A system of psychotherapeutic bodywork found by Alexander Lowen, who was most directly influenced by the work of Wilhelm Reich. Bioenergetics is based on the interconnection between chronic psychological defense mechanisms such as repressed emotional trauma and rigid muscular tension. The tension, known as "armoring," causes severe energy blockage in the body. Exercise, breathing, and psychotherapeutic emotional release techniques are used to release these physical and emotional blocks.

BreathWork:* In its simplest form, this term implies consciously directed breathing techniques for physical, mental or spiritual health. For example, calm methodical breathing is used for calming and relaxation, and forceful breathing for emotional release. Forms of breath work include Rebirthing, Holotropic Breathing, Essential Breathing, Middledorf, Vivation, and Optimal Breathing.

Chakra:*** The word "chakra" (or as it is spelled in Sanskrit— Çakra—with the *c* pronounced as *ch*) means wheel and originally referred to a chariot wheel. Later it became associated with the term "wheel of light" which is the modern usage of the word. The seven chakras were first described nearly 2,600 years ago in the ancient sacred texts. Most of the current Western knowledge of the chakra colors comes from an English translation of Sanskrit texts from the tenth and sixteenth centuries. The seven chakras are the root, spleen, solar plexus, heart, throat, brow, and crown chakras. It is interesting to note that the seven chakras described so long ago actually have a basis in anatomy—they correspond to five main nerve ganglia of the spinal column and two areas of the brain (upper and lower). So in effect, in accordance with the chakra definition, they truly are "energy centers"!

Chi, Ki, Qi: These are the Chinese and Japanese words for the vital life force energy that exists in all living things. This is the energy that flows through the energy meridians of the body.

Chi-Gong (or Qi-Gong): Consists of techniques for dealing with human energy flow. In applying these techniques, one employs the use of the human body's chakras and meridians which are the body's focal points and channels through which its qi energy flows. Qi-Gong works the body from the inside outward. It connects the body and spirit, focusing on breathing, concentration, and physical movements.
Qi-Gong is the art of exercising the jing (essence), qi (energy), and shen (spirit). The nucleus of Qi-Gong is the exercise of yi (consciousness) and qi (vital energy). Correct use of these energies results in regulation of the internal functions of the human body. Qi-Gong does this through developing consciousness and respiration, through causing the internal qi to manifest in awareness, and through moving and strengthening the internal qi.

Circular Breathing: This type of breathing is used in the rebirthing process. There is a connected breath process. The goal is to access the feeling without any noticeable pause in the breath cycle—and to have a relaxed exhale with little control. The breath is usually from the mouth.

Consciousness:** A state of awareness in which the individual is oriented to time, place, and person (i.e., is capable of knowing approximately the date, the nature of the environment, his or her name, and other pertinent personal data). Consciousness combines memories and the comprehension of external reality, as well as the person's emotional state and goals he/she wants to attain. It is then as significant part of what is described as "personality" in the most all-inclusive sense.

Devotional Singing: Spiritual singing performed by groups of individuals with the goal of enhancing inner and worldwide peace.

Emotion:** A mental state or feeling such as fear, hate, love, anger, grief or joy arising as a subjective experience rather than as a conscious mental effort. These feelings constitute the drive that brings about the affective or mental adjustment necessary to satisfy instinctive needs. Physiological changes invariable accompany alteration in emotion, but such change may not be apparent to either the person experiencing the emotion or an observer.

Emotional Release: The release of feelings such as rage, grief, terror with the goal of cleansing and healing the self as well as connecting with a spiritual entity.

Fear: An emotion that has impacted an individual in a definitive way caused by hurt and trauma. Thus an unhealthy thought process develops and a false illusion is created that impacts reality. The hurt experience can result in an unconscious instantaneous thought process setting off emotional anxiety caused by the painful past experience and triggered by a similar present one. The individual once again experiences a threat to the self.

Feeling: This is an energy pattern of the body. Feelings can be defined as healthy or unhealthy and can lead to behaviors that are enhancing or self-defeating.

Frozen Needs: We can characterize frozen needs as unfulfilled and emotionally disordered primary and secondary needs of humankind.

Meditation: Focusing upon stilling the mind and coming into harmony with the soul. Mantras in the form of words or sound can be used to achieve the goal of harmony and peace. A human being can experience more clarity in thought and feeling by releasing compulsive thought through developing the power of observing the mind by meditating.

Peer Cocounseling: An approach wherein two or more individuals share a period of time during which they give and receive loving, aware attention to each others' upsets and feelings of distress. The two individuals are of equal status both employing a set structure. Counselors are trained to actively listen.

Primal (Scream) Therapy:* Based on the premise that trauma and unmet needs from early life create pain which are then often repressed, primal therapy allows an individual to relieve and release imprinted hurtful memories through vocal expression of past trauma. Unacknowledged feelings and needs create neuroses by causing us to split off from our real selves as we try to obtain fulfillment in symbolic ways, which can include such physical and emotional symptoms as anxiety, migraines, asthma, heart disease, and cancer.

Rebirthing:* A self-help method using a simple, defined circular breathing technique to achieve a finer awareness of mind, body, and emotions and bring oneself fully into the present moment. In this state, the individual can experience an expanded awareness of previously submerged feelings and sensations. The significance of the use of the breath in this process lies in its profound connection to thoughts, feelings, and memories. Rebirthing often allows us to reexperience the birth trauma, believed to be the source of the resistance, negativity, and feelings of rejection we carry into adult life. Rebirthing allows full surrender to self so that a natural, smooth restructuring may occur, leading to an overall sense of acceptance, renewal, and gratitude for life. The rebirthing process is best learned under the guidance of a trained professional rebirther.

Rebirthing Components: There are several components of rebirthing. They could include birth trauma, unhealthy or negative thoughts resulting from definitive experiences, someone having a death urge, and distress accumulated from past lifetimes. Leonard Orr made reference to these five components

Reflexology:* A science and art based on the theory that the feet, hands, and outer ears are "maps" of the body, and that relaxing touch techniques for applying gentle nurturing pressure to specific "pressure points" found on these extremities can have a positive effect on corresponding organs throughout the body.

Reiki:* "Universal life force energy." Reiki is a scientific method of activating and balancing the life force energy (also known as ki, qi, prana, and chi) present in all living things. Light hand-placement techniques may be used on the body in order to channel energy to organs and glands and align the chakras (energy centers). There are Reiki techniques for lessening emotional and mental distress and chronic and acute physical problems, as well as for achieving spiritual focus and clarity.

This method of health maintenance and disease prevention can be applied to oneself or to others. Reiki can be a valuable addition to the work of chiropractors, massage therapists, nurses, and others for whom the use of light energy is essential or appropriate. It is an ancient hands-on healing modality originally developed by the Tibetans and rediscovered by the Japanese in the nineteenth century.

Synagogue: A traditional house of spiritual worship for those of the Jewish faith.

Taekwondo: The Korean martial art of the hand and the foot used in the protection, self-defense, and spiritual growth of the individual.

T'ai Chi Chih:* A Chinese Taoist martial art form of meditation in movement, combining mental concentration, coordinated breathing, and a series of slow, graceful body movements. T'ai Chi may be practiced for meditative and health purposes or, with increase speed, the movements may be used for self-defense. The practitioner allows the body weight to sink into the center of gravity (the abdomen) and the feet; this relaxes and deepens the breathing, slows the heartbeat, and improves digestion and various other muscular, neurological, glandular, and organic functions.

Trauma:** An emotional or psychological shock that may produce disordered feelings or behavior.

*Based on definitions in New York Naturally, Community Resources for Natural Living.

**Based on definitions found in a copy of *Tabers Cyclopedia Medical Dictionary #18.*

BIBLIOGRAPHY

Beattie, Melody. *Co-Dependent No More*. New York: Harper Collins & Row. 1987.

Bradshaw, John. *Homecoming: Reclaiming and Championing Your Inner Child*. New York: Bantam Doubleday Dell Publishing. 1992.

Eden, Karan, and Keith Yates. *The Complete Idiot's Guide to Tae Kwon Do*. New York: Alpha Books. 1998.

Eknath, Easwaran. *Meditation: A Simple Eight Point Program for Translating Spiritual Ideals into Daily Life*. Tomales, California: Nilgiri Press. 1991.

Engler, Barbara. *Personality Theories*. Boston: Houghton Mifflin Company, 1999.

Fried, Robert. *Breath Connection*. New York: Plenum Press. 1990.

Dougans, Inge. *The Complete Illustrated Guide to Reflexology: Therapeutic Foot Massage for Health and Well-Being*. Boston, MA: Element Publisher. 1996.

Gilman, Michael. *108 Insights into Tai Chi Chuan. A String of Pearls*. Roslindale, MA: Ymaa Publishing. 1998.

Grof, Stanislav. *Adventure of Self-Discovery*. State University of New York: State University of New York Press, Albany, New York. 1988.

Hay, Louise L. *You Can Heal Your Life.* Carson, California: Hay House, Inc. 1987.

Helms, Joseph M. *Acupuncture Energetics: A Clinical Approach for Physicians.* Berkeley, California. Medical Acupuncture Publishing. 1995.

Hendler, Sheldon Saul. *The Oxygen Breakthrough.* New York: William Morrow. 1998.

Hendrix, Harville. *Getting the Love You Want.* New York: Harper & Row Publishers. 1998.g

Holmes, Ernest. *The Science of Mind.* New York: Dodd, Mead and Company. 1938.

Janov, Arthur. *Primal Scream.* Los Angeles, California. Newstar Media. Inc. 1991.

Jackins, Harvey. *The Human Side of Human Beings. The Theory of Re-Evaluation Counseling.* Seattle, Washington: Rational Island Publishers. 1982.

Korns-Stillwater, Michael. *The Celebration Songbook.* (Santa Barbara, California.) Phone 1-805-969-4550.

Kravitz, Judith. *Breathe Deep, Laugh Loudly. The Joy of Transformational Breathing.* INI Free Press.1999.

Leonard, Jim and Laut, Phil. *Rebirthing. The Science of Enjoying All of Your Life.* Hollywood, CA: Trinity Publications. 1983.

Minett, Gunnel. *Breath & Spirit. Rebirthing as a Healing Technique.*

Mehta, Mira, Elaine Collins, and Sue Atkinson. *How to Use Yoga: A Step-By-Step Guide to the Iyengar Method of Yoga for Relaxation, Health and Well-Being.* Berkeley, California. Rodmell Press. 1998.

Orr, Leonard. *The Story of Rebirthing.* December 1990.

Rama, Swami, Rudolph Ballentine, and Alan Hymes. *Science of Breathing.* Himalayan Institute Press. May 1998.

Rand, Willis L. *Reiki the Healing Touch.*

Ray, Sondra. *Celebration of Breath.* Celestial Arts Paperback. 1984.

Sheehy, Gail: *Middletown, America: One Town's Passage from Trauma to Hope.* Westminster, Maryland: Random House. 2003.

Sky, Michael. Breathing: *Expanding Your Power & Energy.* Bear & Company. 1990.

RESOURCES

Acupuncture: American Academy of Medical
Acupuncture
5820 Wilshire Boulevard
Suite 500
Los Angeles, CA. 90036

Anxiety Disorders Association of America
(*www.adaa.org*) lists self-help groups across the United States.

Cancer Control Society: Lorraine Rosenthal
Contact *www.cancercontrolsociety*.com

Conscious Healing Breath Workers

Joel Vorensky: *jVorensky@sciti.com*
1-619-584-8093

Cass Smith and Shama Smith: Sadhana Fellowship
P.O. Box 230604
Encinitas, CA 92024
Phone: 1-760-633-4490

Angela Geary: RScP, *HealingBreath3@cox.net*
1-619-542-0929

Kennedy Carr: *sarvadharma@cox.net*
1-760-809-3251

Chopra Center
Deepak Chopra:
www.chopra.com
1-888-424-6772

Live Organic Foods: Mary Brenda McQueen,
MaryBrenda@aol.com

Meditation: Candace Kienitz, Religious Science Practitioner RScP,
Candy.Kienitz@neighbor.org

Padmacahaya **Foundation:** Gayle Kildebeck, L.Ac.
www.NorthParkAcupuncture.com

Parables: Dr. Julia Taylor, Aardwolf, Inc.
Aardwolfinc@earthlink.net

Performing Artists

Crystal Bowl Healing:
Crystal Bowl Vibrations for Healing
Web site: www.elivia.com
elivia@cybnetworks.net
1-888-482-8856

Functional Sculpture
Karen Kozlow
699 N. Vulcan Ave #132
Encinitas, CA. 92024
1-760-479-9786

Health and Wellness
Vitamins, Minerals, Herbs

Mr. Donald Schmall
Phone: 1-212-337-1633

Mime:

Imagination-Express
Rosemarie@rosemarieballard.com 619-482-8856
Web site: www.ieallaboard.org

Musicians:

Marsha Jeha 760-723-2795
333 S. Juniper Street # 212
Escondido, CA 92025

Michael Stillwater-Korns:
Michael@innerharmony.com
P.O. Box 2428. Novato, CA 94948

Malaya Rider: *sacredsinging@our4elements*

Steve Ducey: *www.steveducey.com*
steve@steveducey.com 619-994-5026

Deva Premal: *www.mitendevapremal.com*
swan@netone.com 303-494-9060

Non-Native American Sacred Sweat Lodge
www.madregrande.org
619-468-3006

Poet/Performing Artist:

Sacha Rana: *SachaRana@aol.com contact voice Mail: 1-858-492-8846*

Reevaluation Cocounseling:
             Personal Counselors Inc.
             719 2nd North
             Seattle, WA 98109
             1-206-284-0311
             Website: RC.ORG
             E-mail: *ircc@rc.org*

Reflexology: American Academy of Reflexology
    606 East Magnolia Boulevard
    Suite B
    Burbank Ca. 91501
    818-841-7741

Reiki: The Center for Reiki Training
    29209 Northwestern Hwy, #592
    Southfield, MI 48034
    810-948-9534 or 1-800-332-8112

Yoga: American Yoga Associate
    513 South Orange Ave
    Sarasota, Fl 34236
    941-953-5859

OTHER RESOURCES

Mental Health Net
www.mentalhelp.net: Award-winning site over seven
thousand resources in the mental health field

Meditation: Insight Meditation Society
1030 Pleasant Street
Barre, MA 01005
508-355-4378

National Self-Help Clearinghouse

365 Fifth Avenue, Suite 3300
New York, N.Y. 10016
1-212-817-1822
www.selfhelpweb.org
www.cmhc.com/selfhelp
Web site puts you in direct contact with self-help groups

**Touch for Health: Touch for Health Kinesiology
Association**
3223 Washington Boulevard Suite 201
Marina Del Rey, CA 90292
1-800-466-8342

Web MD (*www.webmd.com*) provides a vast array of information
about both physical and mental health issues, including
information about psychological treatments, drug therapy and
prevention.

ABOUT THE AUTHOR

Joel Vorensky embodies the understanding that wisdom comes through doing. His first "doing" was a childhood job shoveling snow. Since then he has worked as a typist; as a taxicab driver in New York City and San Diego, California; as a stevedore (longshoreman) on the docks in Scandinavia; as a teacher of both adults and children in private and public schools in the United States and abroad; and as a retail salesman; registered securities representative; bank officer; insurance broker; publishing; senior public health advisor, immunization and communicable diseases; bookkeeper; beekeeper; baker; agricultural laborer; crowd control officer; ice cream cashier; hospital, liquor, and mailroom clerk; and restaurant busboy.

Teaching and peer counseling (integrative emphasis) has been a consistent theme in his life: languages (English as a Second Language, Swedish, Spanish, and Hebrew) as well as medical terminology, computer software, and marketing. He has taught at the American Language Institute at San Diego State University, national university, and in adult detention centers. Mr. Vorensky has a thirty-three-year background as a peer cocounselor in English and Scandinavian languages.

Joel grew up in Queens, Brooklyn, and New York City. He lived in Scandinavia for seven years and spent several years in the state of Israel living in the desert. For the past eighteen years he has made his home in San Diego, California. He has a daughter, now grown.

Since 1968 he has been on a conscious path to heal the pain that began in the trauma of his birth, a path that has taken him on an odyssey through the various personal growth and healing modalities available in the Eastern and Western world.

Joel holds a degree in business, Scandinavian teaching certification in early childhood and a California teaching credentials in multiple subjects and community college.

Joel is presently obtaining his master's degree in counseling psychology.

The eclectic nature of his experience has afforded him social exposure leading to significant insights as to "what makes people tick." In his second book he freely shares his wisdom with all who care to listen and apply it to the task of improving their own lives.

ORDER FORM

Please send me ____ copies of
I Dare to Heal with Spiritual Power,
hard cover $31.99, and soft cover $21.99.

Book order: $_____
7.75% sales tax (California orders only): _____
Add Shipping: _____

U.S Orders: $500 for first book, $200 for each additional book
International: $9.00 for first book, $5.00 for each additional book
Total: _____

☐ My check/money order for $_____is enclosed.

Please charge my ☐ Visa ☐ Master Card ☐ Discover Card

Account Number _____

Expiration Date _____

Name on Card _____

Daytime phone _____

Signature _____

Send to:

Name _____

Address _____

City, State, Zip _____